HOME WITH A HEART

James C. Dobson, PH. D.

ENCOURAGEMENT FOR FAMILIES

HOME
with a
HEART

Tyndale House Publishers, Inc. • Wheaton, Illinois

Library of Congress Cataloging-in-Publication Data

Dobson, James C., date

  Home with a heart ; encouragement for families / by James C. Dobson.

    p. cm.

  This book is compiled from the author's commentaries featured on his radio program, Focus on the family commentary.

  Includes index.

  ISBN 0-8423-1443-1 (hc : alk. paper)

  1. Family—Religious life. 2. Parenting—Religious aspects—Christianity. 3. Christian life. I. Title.

BV4526.2.D63 1996

248.4—dc21   96-44908

This book is dedicated to the family and to the men, women, and children who live and love within this most basic unit of society. The institutions of marriage and parenthood are vital to the future of humankind. We must give them every opportunity to survive and thrive in an increasingly unfriendly environment. If the commentaries in this book contribute toward that objective in some measure, then my effort in writing them will have been worthwhile.

CONTENTS

▼▼

Thank you for your interest in this little book, *Home with a Heart*. Let me tell you how it came to be written and the purpose for which it is intended.

I have been privileged in recent years to host a daily broadcast aired on 250 of the largest radio and television stations in the United States. The program is also being syndicated in other nations of the world and is expected to reach 50 million people each week in the next year or two. This 90-second feature, called "Focus on the Family Commentary," deals with a wide range of topics related to marriage, parenting, and issues of relevance to the home.

The only difficulty in preparing this program is with its brevity. It is quite a challenge to introduce a topic, to say something useful and interesting about it, and then to hurriedly sign off without exceeding the time limit. Some of you know how tough it is to summarize any thought or idea in a minute and a half. It is actually easier to talk for hours than to speak for only a few moments.

Fortunately, this concise format also imposes a certain discipline on the communicative process. Every word must be chosen with care. Every concept is boiled at high temperature until only that which is pertinent remains. Everything superfluous is eliminated. The final result is a series of recommendations and comments that have been honed and polished to a fine point. The reader will waste no time getting to the heart of the matter.

The book you hold is a compilation of these considered commentaries that we hope will be of interest and help to you. They deal with adolescence, money, sex, the elderly, discipline of children, and dozens of other family-related topics. Some are practical. Some are spiritual. Some are serious. Some are humorous. And some are intended simply to inspire the "better angels" within us. In the end, each commentary is designed to make its own small contribution to the relationships that matter most—those that thrive in the home—where the heart is.

Here's to the health of your family.

—*James C. Dobson, Ph.D.*

WE SOMETIMES LEARN THE MOST from our children.

Some time ago, a friend of mine punished his three-year-old daughter for wasting a roll of gold wrapping paper. Money was tight, and he became infuriated when the child tried to decorate a box to put under the Christmas tree. Nevertheless, the little girl brought the gift to her father the next morning and said, "This is for you, Daddy." He was embarrassed by his earlier over-reaction, but his anger flared again when he found that the box was empty.

He yelled at her, "Don't you know that when you give someone a present, there's supposed to be something inside of it?"

The little girl looked up at him with tears in her eyes and said, "Oh, Daddy, it's not empty. I blew kisses in the box. I filled it with my love. All for you, Daddy."

The father was crushed. He put his arms around his little

girl, and he begged her for forgiveness. My friend told me that he kept that gold box by his bed for years. Whenever he was discouraged, he would take out an imaginary kiss and remember the love of the child who had put it there.

In a very real sense, each of us as parents has been given a gold container filled with unconditional love and kisses from our children. There is no more precious possession anyone could hold.

A Great Cup of Tea

HAVE YOU NOTICED THAT CHILDREN sometimes try to be helpful, but it only makes your life more complicated?

I heard a story about a mother who was sick in bed with the flu. Her darling daughter wanted so much to be a good nurse. She fluffed the pillows and brought a magazine for her mother to read. And then she even showed up with a surprise cup of tea.

"Why, you're such a sweetheart," the mother said as she drank the tea. "I didn't know you even knew how to make tea."

"Oh, yes," the little girl replied. "I learned by watching you. I put the tea leaves in the pan and then I put in the water, and I boiled it, and then I strained it into a cup. But I couldn't find a strainer, so I used the flyswatter instead."

"You what?" the mother screamed.

And the little girl said, "Oh, don't worry, Mom, I didn't use the new flyswatter. I used the old one."

When kids try their hardest and they get it all wrong in spite of themselves, what's a parent to do? What mothers and fathers often do is prevent their children from carrying any responsibility that could result in a mess or a mistake. It's just easier to do everything for them than to clean up afterward. But I urge parents not to fall into that trap.

Your child needs his mistakes. That's how he learns. So go along with the game every now and then . . . even if the tea you drink tastes a little strange.

A Scrawny Cat

I REMEMBER SITTING IN MY CAR at a fast-food restaurant eating a hamburger and French fries, when I happened to look in the rearview mirror. There I saw the most pitiful, scrawny, dirty little kitten on a ledge behind my car. I was so touched by how hungry he looked that I tore off a piece of my hamburger and tossed it to him. But before this kitten could reach it, a huge gray tomcat sprang out of the bushes, grabbed the morsel, and gobbled it down. I felt so sorry for the little guy, who turned and ran back into the shadows, still hungry and frightened.

I was immediately reminded of my years as a junior high school teacher. I saw teenagers every day, who were just as needy, just as deprived, just as lost as that little kitten. It wasn't food that they required; it was love and attention and respect that they needed, and they were desperate for it. And just when they opened up and revealed the pain inside, one of the more popular kids would abuse and ridicule them, sending them scurrying back into the shadows, frightened and alone.

We, as adults, must never forget the pain of trying to grow up and the competitive world in which many adolescents live today. Taking a moment to listen, to care, and to direct such a youngster may be the best investment of a lifetime.

Pachyderms and Teenagers

I ONCE WATCHED A DOCUMENTARY showing how Indian elephants are trained to serve their human masters, and I was struck by the parallel between these beautiful creatures and our fragile teenagers.

The training process for elephants begins shortly after capture with three days of total isolation. These pachyderms are remarkably social animals, and they react to their loneliness in the same way humans do. They grieve and fret and long for their peers. At the peak of their vulnerability, the elephants are brought to a nighttime ceremony of fire where they are screamed at and intimidated for hours. By morning, half-crazed, the elephants have yielded; their wills have been broken. Forever after, they will be slaves to a new master.

We humans also have a great need for love and acceptance, especially during our adolescent years. And like elephants during the night of fire, teenagers are often subjected by their culture to a period of intense isolation and loneliness, which often leaves them feeling rejected, ridiculed, and ignored. Some quickly begin to lose their sense of independence. They become slaves to conformity and peer pressure.

Somehow we must teach our children, long before they are teenagers, that they need not follow the whims of adolescent society. They can lead, or they can follow. It's better to lead.

The Empty Nest

SEVERAL YEARS AGO, OUR YOUNGEST child, Ryan, went off to Chicago for his freshman year of college. His final day at home was filled with the hustle and bustle of packing and getting ready for a new life. Somehow amidst all that activity, the gravity of the evening was missed. But then as we were driving him to the airport the next morning, it dawned on me that parenthood was over. An unexpected wave of grief swept over me. I thought I couldn't stand to see Ryan leave. It wasn't that I wanted to hold him in childhood or to exercise control of his life. No, I mourned the end of an era—a precious time of my life when Ryan and his sister, Danae, were young and their voices rang in the halls of our house. I couldn't hide the tears as we hugged good-bye at Gate 18.

If you're thinking that I'm hopelessly sentimental about my kids, you're right. But I hope my experience encourages those of you whose children are still underfoot. The days that you've been given to care for them are much briefer than you think. Yes, it's a difficult and exhausting assignment, but I urge you to stay the course and finish the job.

By the way, about a month after the departure of our youngest, the empty nest began to look very different to us. The house stayed clean longer, our lives were definitely more tranquil, and my wife and I had more time to enjoy each other. I was reminded of the words of King Solomon, who wrote, "There is a time for everything, and a season for every activity under heaven" (Eccles. 3:1, NIV). That is even true for the task of raising children, and for us, that season has passed.

But if you happen to see my son or daughter, ask them to call home, won't you?

DO FALL AND SPRINGTIME frighten you?

My father was an artist and a poet—not by profession only but also by the beating of his heart—by the very soul of his being. When my mother turned fifty years of age, Dad naturally saw the significance of that milestone and recognized within it the passing of the years and the brevity of life. It inspired him to write a poem that he called, "Your Birthday." These are his words:

The whole world is singing, now that Spring has come.
I saw a robin in the morning sun.
Among the pale green leaves and bursting buds, I heard His talk.
But it is Autumn, where we walk.

'Tis true for us, the Summer too is gone.
Now, whiplash winds arise, and further on
The ice and sleet and cold in grim assault to pierce us through.
Does fall and springtime frighten you?

Impotent shines the April sun so fair,
To melt the wisps of frost within your hair
My dear, I know you feel the threatening gloom but I'm with you
And hand in hand, we'll face the Winter too.

Well, my mother and father did face the winter together. Now they lie side by side on a windswept hill where they once loved to walk. And now my wife and I are experiencing "fall and springtime."

High-Voltage Marriages

WHICH OF THE FOLLOWING COUPLES is more likely to enjoy the greatest physical attraction in their marriage? Is it the couple that spends every waking hour together and focuses almost exclusively on one another, or is it the man and woman who have other interests and then, after some time of independence, come closer together again as the pendulum swings?

Surprisingly, perhaps, it's the one that varies from time to time. According to behavioral researchers, the healthiest marriages and those with the highest sexual voltage are those that "breathe"— relationships that move from a time of closeness and tenderness to a more distant posture and then come together for another reunion as the cycle concludes.

This is why it's not always advantageous for a husband and wife to work together or to concentrate exclusively on one another in the absence of friends and colleagues outside the family. There is something about the diversity of interests and activities by each partner that keeps a couple from consuming one another and burning out the relationship in the short run.

Marriage is, after all, a marathon and not a sprint. Husbands and wives need to maintain a regenerating system that will keep love alive for a lifetime. Cultivating a healthy interest in many things is one big step in that direction.

ONE WRITER ON THE SUBJECT OF child development suggested that parents and children should be on an even playing field—making decisions by negotiation and compromise. After all, he said, who knows what is best for the boy or girl? Maybe the child is right and the parent is wrong.

When I heard that advice, with which I strongly disagree, I was reminded of a little hamster that once belonged to my daughter. One day I sat watching that furry little animal trying to get out of his cage. He worked tirelessly to open the gate and push his furry little nose between the bars. Then I noticed our dachshund, *Siggie*, sitting eight feet away in the shadows. He was watching the hamster, too. His ears were erect, and it was obvious what was on his mind. He was thinking, *Come on, baby. Open that door, and I'll have you for lunch.* If the hamster had been so unfortunate as to escape from his cage, which he desperately wanted to do, he would have been dead in a matter of seconds.

Obviously, I saw something from where I sat that the hamster couldn't have known. I had a different perspective than he did. I was aware of dangers that he couldn't have foreseen. That's why I denied him something that he desperately wanted to achieve.

So it is with children. Parents have the perspective of maturity that their kids lack. Sometimes the very thing they want most would be disastrous if they should be granted it. That's why I am a firm advocate of parental authority when children are young. Even though parents aren't perfect, most of them do what is best for their kids—and we must not undermine their ability to lead in their own homes.

This position is supported unequivocally by Scripture: The apostle Paul wrote, "Children, obey your parents in all things: for this is well pleasing unto the Lord" (Col. 3:20).

The Disease of Materialism

I REMEMBER SEEING AN advertisement from a large bank that encouraged people to borrow money, asking the question: "What do you need to make you happy?" How foolish, I thought, to believe that a new car or a boat or even a house can hold the keys to personal satisfaction.

Materialism is a disease that infects the human family—and it's not a problem only in affluent cultures. Author and financial counselor Ron Blue tells the story of visiting a small, rural village in Africa. Ron asked a native there what was the biggest problem facing his village. The man said, "Materialism."

Ron was taken aback. He expected it to be the lack of food or medical attention, or perhaps problems with neighboring villages. But materialism? These villagers didn't have televisions or cars or satellite dishes—the sorts of things we associate with "the good life." But this villager told Ron, "If a man has a mud hut, he wants one made out of cow manure. If he has a cow manure hut, he wants a stone hut. If he has a thatch roof, he wants a tin roof. If he has one acre, he wants two. Materialism is a disease of the heart. It has nothing to do with where you live."

That's probably the simplest and best explanation of materialism I've heard. And it might hit pretty close to where you live.

Take a good hard look at the loved ones in your life—and then tell me where your real priorities are.

MANY YEARS AGO, A FOUR-YEAR-OLD
girl named Sandra Louise Doty sat on a stool in a florist's shop
while her grandmother made arrangements for customers. As
the grandmother and granddaughter chatted, the child began
describing what she thought a grandmother was like. The older
woman wrote down Sandra's words, which have been quoted
around the world. Sandra is now Mrs. Andrew De Mattia,
and has given us permission to share with you her original
composition entitled, "What a Grandmother Is." [1]

The little girl said, "A grandmother is a lady who has no
children of her own, so she likes other people's little girls. A
grandfather is a man grandmother. He goes for walks with the
boys, and they talk about fishing and tractors and like that.
Grandmas don't have to do anything except be there. They're
old, so they shouldn't play hard or run. It is enough if they drive
us to the market where the pretend horse is and have lots of dimes

ready. Or if they take us for walks, they should slow down past things like pretty leaves or caterpillars. They should never, ever say hurry up.

"Usually, they are fat, but not too fat to tie kids' shoes. They wear glasses and funny underwear. They can take off their teeth and gums. They don't have to be smart, only answer questions like why dogs hate cats and how come God isn't married? They don't talk baby talk like visitors do, because it is hard to understand. When they read to us they don't skip or mind if it is the same story again."

Then she finished, "Everybody should try to have [a grandmother], especially if you don't have television, because grandmas are the only grown-ups who have got time."

Sandra has told us what children value most in adults: one who is kind, appreciates the finer things of life, and isn't too busy to love a kid.

RECENTLY I HEARD AN INCREDIBLE story of the perseverance of Pacific salmon from a nature video produced by the Moody Institute of Science. A salmon was spawned in a hatchery in northern California, released into a channel which led to a stream, the stream to a river, and the river to the Pacific Ocean. After becoming ocean-bound, the fish swam thousands of miles. Then, as if by command, she began a treacherous journey back to the place of her spawning. The fish relocated not only the spot where she'd entered the ocean but the river, the stream, and the exact inlet from which she had been released.

Now, here's the almost unbelievable part of the story. The salmon worked her way up through a drain and pushed through a heavy screened lid on top of a three-foot vertical pipe, all to end up in the very same tank from which she was hatched. Special markings on her fin confirmed the amazing journey.

As I thought about this feat, it occurred to me that there is, perhaps, a parallel between the early life of the salmon and the impact we, as parents, have on our children. Our kids are shaped forever by the love and training received at home. They will always be influenced by the experiences that characterized the family in which they were raised. Not one experience is ever completely lost. Even at fifty years of age, they will "remember" and be guided by that which was taught in childhood. It's an awesome thought.

IMAGINE THE AGONY A SINGLE parent goes through when required by court order to put his or her children on an airplane, all alone, for an extended visitation with the other parent.

One single mom described her feelings. She said:

"I stand in the terminal, and I watch the kids' airplane disappear into the clouds. I feel an incredible sense of loss. The loneliness immediately starts to set in. I worry constantly about their safety, but I resist the urge to call every hour to see how they're doing. And when they do call me to tell me how much fun they're having, I grieve over the fact that they're living a life completely separate from my own. My only consolation is knowing that they're coming home soon. But I'm haunted by the fear that they won't want to come home with me."

For the single parent who identifies with this hurting mother, there may be a way to get through the painful days of waiting.

Instead of seeing this time alone as a period of isolation and deprivation, view it as an opportunity to recharge the batteries and reinvigorate the spirit. Spend some uninterrupted time with friends. Read an inspirational book, or return to a hobby that you've set aside. Fill your day with things that are impossible amidst the responsibility of child care, recognizing that your children will benefit from your rehabilitation. They'll return to a reenergized parent, instead of one coming off weeks of depression.

Children and Exercise

A RECENT MEDICAL STUDY conducted at Columbia Children's Hospital in Ohio has confirmed that today's children are heavier and have significantly higher cholesterol and triglyceride levels than kids did even fifteen years ago. One of the researchers, Dr. Hugh Allens, said, "Unless these trends change, 30 million of the 80 million children alive today in the United States will eventually die of heart disease."[2]

Dr. Allens said, "Kids need to turn off the TV, get off the couch." The problem is that high-fat junk food has replaced good nutrition. And even when healthy foods are consumed, kids are not exercising the calories off. Between television, car pools, computer games, and just hanging out at the pizza parlor, kids just don't run and jump like they used to.

So Mom and Dad should find energetic activities to do together with kids. Things like walking and bicycling and playing catch, or hiking. Parents can also get their children involved in community or school sports programs, ranging from softball to soccer.

Children are busy forming habits for a lifetime, so eating right and exercising every day will contribute to greater health in the future. And once your children are on the right path, you might want to begin working on yourself.

A Star in the Apple

SOME PARENTS REFER TO THEIR children as the "apple" of their eye, but one mom I know affectionately thinks of her kids as the "star" in the apple.

This mother discovered one day that by cutting an apple horizontally across the middle, instead of coring it and slicing it in wedges from top to bottom, that something new and striking appeared. A perfect five-point star was formed by the tiny seeds at the center. The star had been there all along, of course, but she'd just never seen it before because she always approached the apple from a different point of view.

There's an analogy to children here that intrigues me. Most of us look at these little creatures we call kids in a certain way year after year. We see them perhaps as lazy or irritating or demanding. But children are infinitely complex, and we may be overlooking qualities of character that we've never seen before. We could be missing the "star" at the heart of these young lives.

If we try to see them through fresh eyes every now and then, we may stumble onto a whole new wonderful dimension to their personalities that escaped us before. So give it a try! Begin looking at your children from a new angle.

There is, I promise, a star tucked away inside every boy and girl.

SHELTERING A CHILD FROM THE consequences of his or her behavior could help create an immature adult later.

One of the prime objectives during the preadolescent years is to teach a child that behavior leads inevitably to consequences. Unfortunately, that connection is often interrupted. For example, a seven-year-old begs for a dog but is never asked to feed and care for him. A ten-year-old is caught stealing candy from a store, but he's released to the custody of his parents. Nothing happens. A fifteen-year-old takes the keys to the family car, but the parents pay the fine for her driving without a license. So all through childhood, such loving parents, in their misguided efforts to shield the child from pain, have stood between his or her behavior and the natural consequences that flow from it. Under these circumstances, a young person may enter adulthood not really knowing that life can bite. He or she may become a grown-up adolescent constantly needing someone to bail him or her out of trouble.

How does one avoid this blunder? By linking behavior to consequences. If Jane carelessly loses her lunch money, she just may have to skip a meal. If Jack misses the school bus because he dawdled in the morning, he may have to walk to school.

Now obviously, it would be easy to carry this principle too far and become harsh. But a taste of bitter fruit that irresponsibility brings can teach a youngster valuable lessons that may be useful later on.

Beating Burnout

I TALK TO MANY MOTHERS THESE days, especially those with younger kids, who feel like they're on the edge of burnout. They feel like they will explode if they have to do one more load of laundry or tie one more shoe. Their circumstances are very different than those their grandmothers, who typically had extended families and neighbors to help them raise their kids, faced. They were surrounded by mothers, aunts, sisters, and friends who provided encouragement, advice, and support in times of need.

But in today's mobile, highly energized society, young mothers are much more isolated and lonely. Many of them hardly know the women next door, and their sisters and mothers may live a thousand miles away. That's why it is so important for those with small children to stay in touch with the outside world. Though it may seem safer and less taxing to remain cloistered within the four walls of a home, it is a mistake to do so.

Loneliness does bad things to the mind. Furthermore, there are many ways to network with other women today, including church activities, Bible study groups, and support programs, such as "Moms In Touch, International" and "Mothers of Preschoolers."

Husbands of stay-at-home mothers need to recognize the importance of their support, too. It is a wise man who plans a romantic date at least once a week and offers to take care of the children so Mom can get a much-needed break.

In short, burnout is not inevitable even in a busy household. It can be avoided in families that recognize its symptoms and take steps to head it off.

It's the Simple Things That Count

YOU DON'T HAVE TO SPEND HUGE amounts of money to have a meaningful family life. Children love the most simple, repetitive kinds of activities. They want to be read the same stories hundreds of times and hear the same jokes long after they've heard the punch lines. These interactions with parents are often more fun than expensive toys or special events.

A friend of mine once asked his grown children what they remembered most fondly from their childhood. Was it the vacations they took together or the trips to Disney World or the zoo? No, they told him. It was when he would get on the floor and wrestle with the four of them. They would gang-tackle the "old man" and laugh until their sides hurt. That's the way children think. The most meaningful activities within families are often those that focus on that which is spontaneous and personal.

This is why you can't buy your way out of parenting responsibilities, though many have tried. Busy and exhausted mothers and fathers, especially those who are affluent, sometimes attempt to "pay off" their deprived kids with toys, cars, and expensive experiences. It rarely works. What boys and girls want most is time spent with their parents—building things in the garage or singing in the car or hiking to an old fishing pond. No toy, to be played with alone, can ever compete with the enjoyment of such moments. And those moments will be remembered for a lifetime.

Sunday, a Day of Rest

REMEMBER WHEN THE WORLD seemed to slow down on Sundays?

Monday through Friday were for work and school. Saturday was for chores. And Sunday . . . well, Sunday was a quieter day when things geared down for the world to catch its breath. But with the passage of time, Sunday began to lose its significance. Now we huff and puff seven days a week, hurtling down the road toward burnout or even an early demise. I'd like to make a case once more for setting aside one day per week for rest, relaxation, and worship.

I've recently been privileged to spend some time with Truett Cathy, the founder and CEO of the Chick-Fil-A restaurant corporation. When he began his business in the 1950s, he determined that he would close all of his stores on Sunday, regardless of the circumstances. Then it was an accepted practice. Now it's extremely unusual, especially for a restaurant chain with many outlets in malls. To this day, Cathy has never wavered from his commitment. He told me he believes Sunday is a special day, a day set apart from the rest of the week.

Sound old-fashioned? Well, perhaps. But maybe it's one traditional idea that still has a place today. Why don't you try gearing down just a bit this next Sunday? The fourth commandment instructs us to do just that.

View from the Emergency Room

MANY OF US KNOW THE TRAUMA of rushing our young ones off to the local emergency room for trauma care. We usually encounter crowded waiting rooms and frustrating forms to fill out, and all the while we're wondering, "What's wrong with my child?" and "How bad is he or she hurt?"

A typical inner-city emergency room will see about four thousand patients per month. While you and I are sleeping peacefully at 2 A.M., the emergency room can be a hubbub of activity—with anything from people who have merely cut themselves while washing dishes to victims of serious car accidents or crime. Medical teams attempt as best they can to meet each patient's needs within a few critical minutes.

My friend, emergency-room physician Dr. Elsburg Clark, has been alarmed over the past few years by the growing number of patients, especially children, whose lives are endangered by household drugs, poisonous chemicals, unsupervised swimming pools, and accidental shootings. Many times he has had the unenviable task of telling families that their little one is not going to come home. It's made him much more protective of his own kids, and he strongly suggests basic things that parents can do to help avoid medical emergencies.

It's not new advice, but we need to hear it again. Lock away all medicines, chemicals, and flammable substances. Get rid of slippery rugs and wobbly ladders. Build strong fences around swimming pools, and secure the gate above the reach of young children. And by all means, unload all guns and keep them under lock and key.

Let's make our homes safe havens in which our boys and girls can grow in safety.

You Don't Trust Me

IF THERE'S A MAGIC BULLET THAT teenagers use to manipulate their folks, it's these four words: You don't trust me!

The instant a young person accuses us of being suspicious and imagining the worst, we start backpedaling. "No, dear, it's not that I don't trust you being out with your friends or taking the car, it's just that I . . . ," and then we run out of words. We're on the defensive, and the discussion is over.

Well, maybe it's time we recognized that trust is divisible. In other words, we can trust our children at some things but not at others. It's not an all-or-nothing proposition. This is the way the world of business works from day to day. Many of us are authorized, for example, to spend our company's money from certain accounts but not the whole corporate checkbook. I don't trust myself to attempt certain things like skydiving or bungee jumping, for another example.

So let's stop being suckered by our kids and boldly state that trust comes in stages. Some of it now and more later on.

Parents have the task of risking only what we can reasonably expect to be handled safely. To do more is not really trust; it's foolhardiness.

The Great Condom Caper

YOUNG PEOPLE ARE BEING TOLD today that they can have sex with numerous partners if they will simply "protect themselves" by using condoms. It sounds simple, doesn't it? What does medical science tell us about the effectiveness of these devices?

A careful investigation revealed that condoms failed to prevent pregnancy among married couples 15.7 percent of the time.[3] Another study showed that they failed 36 percent of the time in preventing pregnancy among young unmarried minority women.[4] This dismal record explains why there's a word for people who rely on condoms as a means of birth control. We call them *parents*.

Now remember that a woman can conceive only two or three days per month, whereas HIV and other sexually transmitted diseases (STDs) can be transmitted 365 days per year. If condoms are not used properly, if they are defective, or if they slip just once, the results can be disastrous. One mistake after hundreds of protected episodes is all it takes to catch an STD. The young victim who's told by his or her elders that this little latex device makes intercourse "safe" may not know what lies ahead. Lifelong pain and even death are being risked for a brief moment of pleasure. What a burden to place on an immature mind and body!

The only way to protect yourself from deadly diseases is to practice abstinence as long as you are single, then marry an uninfected person (if you marry at all), and live together in mutual fidelity for life. That is the biblical plan—and it is the only behavior that makes sense during an epidemic of STDs.

Through the Darkness

I'M TOLD THAT WHEN I WAS A very small child—maybe two years of age—my family lived in a one-bedroom apartment, and my little bed was located beside the bed of my parents. My father said that it was common during that time for him to awaken at night to a little voice that was whispering, "Daddy? Daddy? Daddy?"

My father would answer quietly, "What, Jimmy?"

And I would say, "Hold my hand!"

My dad would reach across the darkness and grope for my little hand, finally engulfing it in his. He said later that the instant he had my hand firmly in his grip, my arm would become limp and my breathing deep and regular. I would immediately fall back to sleep.

You see, I only wanted to know that he was there! Until the day he died, I continued to reach for him—for his assurance, for his guidance—but mostly just to know that he was there.

Then, so very quickly, I found myself in my dad's place. And I wanted to be there for my children—not just a name on their birth certificate, but a strong, warm, and loving presence in their lives.

You see, a dad occupies a place in a child's heart that no one else can satisfy. So to all the men out there who are blessed to be called fathers: I urge you to be there for the little ones in your life who call you "Dad."

Two Kinds of Kids

HAVE YOU NOTICED THERE ARE TWO kinds of kids in the world? Yes, there are boys and girls, but they differ in another important way, too. We can divide them into two categories according to their basic temperaments.

The first is composed of "compliant kids," those who sleep through the night from the second week of life. They coo at their grandparents, and they smile while their diapers are being changed. They never spit up on the way to the grocery store or the doctor's office because that would be inconvenient for their parents. During later childhood they love to keep their rooms clean and they do their homework brilliantly without being asked.

Then there are the children we might call "strong-willed" kids. They get their mother's attention long before birth because they start scratching their initials on the walls and kicking like crazy. They enter the world smoking a cigar, yelling about the temperature in the delivery room, and complaining about the utter incompetence of the nursing staff. From about eighteen months forward, they want to run things and tell everyone else what to do. Their favorite word is "no!"

Compliant children are a breeze to raise, of course, but the tougher kids can turn out fine, too. The trick is to shape that strong will during the early years without breaking the spirit. This is done by setting boundaries very clearly and then enforcing them with loving firmness. Even the toughest kids find security in a structured environment where other people's rights, as well as their own, are protected. That task is one of the most important challenges of parenthood.

When it is done right, even the most independent child can learn to be responsible and self-disciplined.

Fathers and the Empty Nest

WHEN WE HEAR THE PHRASE "empty nest" we often think of mothers who are going through pain and depression as their children move away. But research shows that fathers feel the pain as well—in many cases even more intensely than their wives.

The movie *Father of the Bride* is hilarious. But it's also a touching tribute to the love of a father for his daughter. When George, the dad, sits across from his daughter at the dinner table and learns that she's engaged, he takes the news hard. He can't believe what he's hearing. He has to clear his vision as he sees her as a little baby girl, and then as the tomboy of eight or ten years, and finally as a beautiful young woman of eighteen. His little girl has grown up, and she's leaving him. He will never again be main man in the life of this baby or this little girl or this beautiful young adult. A part of his life is over, and there's grieving to be done.

George's experience is not so unusual. A recent study asked four hundred parents of college freshmen to report their feelings when their son or daughter left home. Surprisingly to some, the fathers took it harder than the mothers. And one of the chief explanations was regret. Fathers had been so busy—working so hard—that they suddenly realized it was too late to build a relationship with the then-grown child.

For those of you who still have teenagers at home, take a moment regularly to enjoy your remaining time together. Those days will be gone in the blink of an eye.

The Class Clown

I'LL BET YOU REMEMBER HIM—
the kid who could make everyone crack up at the most inopportune
times? He was a trial to his teachers, an embarrassment to his
parents, and an utter delight to every child who wanted to escape the
boredom of school. And there are millions of them on the job today.
It's my belief that boards of education assign at least one clown to
every class to make sure that schoolteachers earn every dollar of their
salaries.

These skilled little disrupters are usually boys. They often
have reading or other academic problems. They may be small in
stature, although not always, and they'll do anything for a laugh.
Their parents and teachers may not recognize that behind the
boisterous behavior is often the pain of inferiority.

You see, humor is a classic response to feelings of low self-
esteem. That's why within many successful comedians is the
memory of a hurting little boy or girl. Jonathan Winters's

parents were divorced when he was seven years old, and he said he used to cry when he was alone because other children teased him about not having a father. Joan Rivers frequently jokes about her unattractiveness as a girl. She says she was such a dog her father had to throw a bone down the aisle to get her married. And so it goes.

These and other comedians got their training during childhood, using humor as a defense against childhood hurts. That's also the inspiration for the class clown. By making an enormous joke out of everything, he conceals the self-doubt that churns inside.

Understanding that should help us meet his needs and manage him more effectively.

Sending the Roots Down Deep

CONTRARY TO WHAT SOME PARENTS may believe, the ideal environment for a child is not one devoid of problems and trials.

Though it's hard to accept at the time, your children need the minor setbacks and disappointments that come their way. How can they learn to cope with problems and frustrations if their early experiences are totally without trial? Nature tells us so. A tree that's planted in a rain forest is never forced to extend its roots downward in search of water. Consequently, it remains poorly anchored and can be toppled by even a moderate wind. By contrast, a mesquite tree that's planted in a dry desert is threatened by its hostile environment. It can only survive by sending its roots down thirty feet or more into the earth, seeking cool water. But through this adaptation to an arid land, the well-rooted tree becomes strong and steady against all assailants.

Our children are like the two trees in some ways. Those who

have learned to conquer their problems are better anchored than those who have never faced them.

Our task as parents, then, is not to eliminate every challenge for our children. Rather, it is to serve as a confident ally on their behalf, encouraging them when they're distressed, intervening when the threats become overwhelming, and "being there" when the crises come. Above all, we need to give them the tools with which to overcome the inevitable obstacles of life.

Inexplicable Behavior

A VERY PUZZLED MOTHER ONCE asked me, "Why is it that some kids with every advantage and opportunity seem to turn out bad, while others raised in terrible homes become pillars of the community?" It's a good question.

I stood there nodding my head as this mother went on to tell stories of neglectful and couldn't-care-less parents who somehow raised model citizens. I could've cited a number of examples myself, because the fact is, environment simply doesn't account for everything. There's something else within us that makes us who we are. Some behavior is caused, and some plainly isn't. Remember that the same boiling water that softens the carrot also hardens the egg. Likewise, some youngsters react positively to certain circumstances while others react negatively. We don't know why.

What we do know is that children are more than the sum total of their experiences. They're more than the product of their nutrition or even their genetic inheritance. They are certainly more than their parents' influence. They are uniquely crafted individuals, every one of them, and they're capable of independent and rational thought that's not attributable to any source. That's what makes them human, and that's what also makes the task of parenting so challenging but also so rewarding. We don't need to take all the blame when they go wrong, but neither should we take the full credit when they excel.

Get 'Em Organized!

WHAT IS THE PRIMARY REASON for failure in high school? The answer may surprise you.

According to educational consultant Cheri Fuller, the chief problem is not laziness or poor study skills. No, the main reason for poor school performance is disorganization. "Show me a student's notebook," Fuller says, "and I'll tell you whether that individual is a B student or a D student." An achieving student's notebook is arranged neatly with dividers and folders for handouts and assignments. A failing student's notebook is usually a jumbled mess and may not even be used at all.

Some children are naturally sloppy, but most of them can learn to be better organized. Fuller says this skill should be taught during the elementary school years. Once they enter junior high, students may have as many as five teachers, each assigning different textbooks, workbooks, handouts, and assignments from various classroom subjects. It is foolish to assume that kids who have never had any organizational training will be able to keep such detail straight and accessible. If we want them to function in this system, we need to give them the tools that are critical to success.

Organization! It's one very important key to success in school.

Children Having Children

WHAT SHOULD PARENTS DO WHEN a teenage daughter comes to them and speaks those electrifying words, "Mom and Dad, I'm pregnant"?

Responding to a teen pregnancy is one of the most difficult trials parents are ever asked to face. When the news breaks, it's reasonable to feel anger toward the girl who has brought this problem into their lives. How dare this kid do something so stupid and hurtful to herself and the entire family!

Once Mom and Dad have caught their breath, however, a more rational and loving response is appropriate. This is no time for recriminations. Their daughter needs understanding and guidance now more than ever, and they are the ones to provide it. She'll face many important decisions in the next few months, and she'll need a calm, rational, and caring mother and father to assist in determining the best path to take.

If parents can call up that kind of strength, they and their daughter will eventually enjoy the bond that often develops between people who have survived a crisis together.

Dad As the Interpreter of Mom

WHERE DO CHILDREN LEARN TO think highly of their mothers? Who sets the pattern for their young minds, positioning Mom as a much loved and respected member of the family—instead of being chief cook and scrub lady?

The best public-relations agent for Mom—is Dad. Fathers can wield tremendous influence over what children think of their mothers, or of women in general. Early in my marriage to Shirley, I learned that occasional irritation between us quickly reflected itself in the behavior of our children. They seemed to feel, "If Dad can argue with Mom, then we can, too." I learned how important it was to express love and admiration for my wife, even when there were issues that we needed to iron out beyond their gaze. In short, my attitudes became the attitudes of my children, which I now know to be typical.

In a world that often discounts the contribution of women, especially homemakers, it's up to us as husbands to say in a dozen ways, "Your mother is a wonderful woman! She works hard and she deserves tremendous credit for what she gives to us all. As far as I'm concerned, she's number one!"

Kids will quickly recognize the respect shown by a father and reflect it in their attitudes and behavior. It is a public-relations assignment that only they can perform.

IS DAD THOUGHT OF AS A HERO OR a bum in his home? The answer probably depends on what Mom thinks.

This maternal influence is powerfully expressed in the book *Fathers and Sons*, by Lewis Yablonsky. He told about sitting around the dinner table listening to his mother say things like, "Look at your father! His shoulders are bent down; he's a failure. He doesn't have the courage to get a better job or make more money. He's a beaten man."

Yablonsky's father never defended himself. He just kept staring at his plate. As a result, his three sons grew up believing their father really was a wimp. They never noticed his virtues or the fact that he did indeed work hard to support his family.

Yablonsky concluded with this statement, "My overall research clearly supports that the mother is the basic filter and has enormous significance on the father-son relationship." I strongly agree. How much better for a wife to praise her husband, to point out his strengths, to position him in the children's eyes as someone with courage and principles.

Mom's going to need the influence of a strong man in the lives of her children. She would do well to contribute to their image of him as a leader.

THERE'S A CLASSIC POEM BY Eugene Field called "Little Boy Blue" that my father used to quote to me when I was a child, and it made me cry. It had great meaning for me then, even as a youngster, but the words took on new significance when I became a father.

Let me share it with you today.

> The little toy dog is covered with dust,
> But sturdy and staunch he stands;
> And the little toy soldier is red with rust,
> And the musket moulds in his hands.
> Time was when the little toy dog was new,
> And the soldier was passing fair;
> And that was the time when our Little Boy Blue
> Kissed them and put them there.
>
> "Now, don't you go till I come," he said,
> "And don't you make any noise!"

So, toddling off to his trundle-bed,
He dreamt of the pretty toys;
And, as he was dreaming, an angel song
Awakened our Little Boy Blue
Oh! the years are many, the years are long,
But the little toy friends are true!

Aye, faithful to Little Boy Blue they stand,
Each in the same old place
Awaiting the touch of a little hand
The smile of a little face;
And they wonder, as waiting the long years through
In the dust of that little chair,
What has become of our Little Boy Blue,
Since he kissed them and put them there.
(Copyright © 1932 by Julia S. Field)

This poem is dedicated to those mothers and fathers who have lost a child in recent years. My prayers are with you.

CHILDREN INEVITABLY BECOME angry with their parents from time to time. Should they be allowed to express that emotion, and if so, precisely how?

If a child is prohibited from expressing his or her negative frustrations toward mother or father, that individual will often vent those feelings through what psychologists call "passive aggression." Maybe he'll pout or wet the bed or get bad grades in school. Perhaps she'll become depressed or eat too much. Usually children aren't aware that these behaviors are being fueled by anger. The behaviors are simply unconscious ways of expressing accumulated hostility toward parents.

It *is* important, therefore, to allow children to vent anger when it is intense. On the other hand, I firmly believe that they should also be taught to be respectful to their parents. It is not appropriate to permit name-calling, back talk, or sassiness and disrespect. Instead, children should be assured that they can say anything to their parents, including very negative feelings, as long as it's expressed in a respectful manner.

For example, "You embarrassed me in front of my friends," or, "I don't think I got my fair share," or, "Sometimes I think you love Billy more than me." Those are appropriate responses. "I hate you" and "You are so stupid!" are not acceptable retorts.

By following this general guideline, we're teaching children how to deal with anger in appropriate ways. That skill might come in handy with a future husband or wife.

Temper Tirades

EVERYONE WHO HAS RAISED A toddler has probably been confronted at some point by a full-blown temper tantrum. Its fury is something to behold coming from a kid who only weighs twenty-five pounds. Usually a firm hand will discourage such violent behavior—but sometimes not. Some children throw tantrums specifically for the purpose of stirring up and manipulating the big powerful adults who claim to be in charge.

I knew one family, for example, that had a three-year-old boy who was still throwing the most terrible fits when he didn't get his way. He would fall on the floor—kick, scream, spit, and cry. His parents had done everything they knew to stop the tantrums, with no success. One night, they were reading the paper when the kid wanted them to do something. They didn't move quickly enough, so he went into his violent contortions. Out of exasperation, since the parents didn't know what else to do, they didn't do anything. They just went on reading. The child was shocked by their unresponsiveness. He got up, went over to his mother, shook her arm, and again fell screaming to the floor. Still neither parent reacted. He then approached his father and hit the newspaper before going into another tirade. By this point, Mom and Dad were secretly watching to see what would happen, but they remained passive. This kid felt so foolish and stupid throwing temper tantrums with no audience—that I never threw another one.

The next time your toddler goes a little crazy—you might try doing nothing. It worked in at least one case with which I am quite familiar.

After the Fight Is Over

IT'S NOT THE FIGHTS THAT SHOULD worry married couples; it's what happens when the battles are over.

Almost all husbands and wives experience conflict from time to time, which is not necessarily unhealthy to their relationships. A verbal spat that stays within reasonable limits can open the windows and give the couple a chance to vent frustrations and release some steam. The important question, however, is what happens after a fight is over? In healthy relationships, a period of confrontation ends in forgiveness, in drawing together, in deeper respect and understanding, and sometimes in sexual satisfaction. But in unstable marriages, conflict is never entirely resolved. This is a very dangerous situation, where the consequences of one battle begin to overlap with a prelude to the next. It's a good idea for couples to take a close look at what happens in the aftermath of confrontation.

Are there things that you've said or done that have grieved your partner? Do you need to ask forgiveness for attacking the self-worth of your spouse instead of focusing on the issues that divided you? Are there substantive matters that haven't yet been resolved? Deal with them quickly before they can fester and erode the relationship from within.

The apostle Paul understood this principle clearly. He instructed us not to let the sun go down on our wrath (Eph. 4:26). That's great marital advice.

Fathers and Daughters

LONG BEFORE A TEENAGE GIRL finds her first real boyfriend or falls in love, her attitude toward men has been shaped quietly by her father. Why? Because the father-daughter relationship sets the stage for all future romantic involvement.

If a young woman's father is an alcoholic and a bum, she'll spend her life trying to find a man who can meet the needs her father never fulfilled in her heart. If he's warm and nurturing, she'll look for a lover to equal him. If he thinks she's beautiful and feminine, she'll be inclined to see herself that way. But if he rejects her as unattractive and uninteresting, she's likely to carry self-image problems into her adult years.

I've also observed that a woman's relationship with her future husband is significantly influenced by the way she perceived her father's authority. If he was overbearing or capricious during her earlier years, she may be inclined to precipitate power struggles with her husband throughout married life. But if Dad blended love and discipline in a way that conveyed strength, she may be more comfortable with a give-and-take marriage characterized by mutual respect.

So much of what goes into marriage starts with a girl's father. That's why it behooves us as dads to give our best effort to the raising of those kids around our feet.

An Elderly Woman Speaks

SOME YEARS AGO, JEANIE ROEMER was a guest on a Focus on the Family radio program to discuss the subject of caring for elderly parents. During that broadcast, she quoted from a letter written by her mother, Mom Keltner. Mrs. Keltner was approaching eighty years old when this letter was written, and its content surprised her family because they hadn't been aware of her feelings and her needs. Here is a portion of that letter:[5]

I hate having to rely on my children to do things for me that I could do for myself a few years ago. The truth of it is that our roles are reversed now, and I am your child needing you in a special way. I need your patience now when I don't hear what you say the first time; so please don't be annoyed. I need your patience when I think too much about the past. I need your patience with my slowness and my set ways.

I want you to be tolerant with what the years have done to me physically. And please, be understanding about my personal care habits. I really can't see when my dress is dirty or the floor needs cleaning. I spill things. I lose things. I get unduly excited when I try to figure out my bank statements. I can't remember what time to take my medication, or if I took it already. I am simply so slow. I can't seem to move fast anymore, and that bothers me as much as it does you. Try to understand; some days I don't feel like getting dressed, and that's the reason I'm still in my robe at noon on those days. I take too many naps, I know, because you have said, "Quit spending all of your time sleeping." Well, sometimes, sleep helps to pass the day. When I have nothing but time on my hands, a 15-minute nap seems like an hour.

Finally, [the apostle] Paul wrote, "I can do all things through Christ which strengtheneth me." I know I can, too! Maybe I can't do all I want to, the way I used to, but how comforting it is to know I don't have to rely solely on myself. It's a wonderful feeling to know his eye is on the sparrow, and I know he cares for me. I guess being eighty isn't so bad after all. God has blessed me so much.

Love, Mom Keltner

Could there be an elderly member of your family who has thoughts similar to those written by Mom Keltner? Within every aging body is a breathing, feeling human being, who needs to be loved and understood as the ravages of time take their toll.

Keeping the Brain Healthy

DID YOU HEAR ABOUT THE NINETY-
four-year-old man who went to the doctor because his hip was
aching? The doctor examined him and said, "Well, what do you
expect? You're ninety-four years old!" The man replied, "Well,
how come my other hip doesn't know that?"

Is it possible to grow old without parts of our body—especially
our brain—wearing out? Specifically, are there techniques for
remaining mentally alert as we age? An article in *Family Circle*
magazine suggested five ways to maintain healthy minds through
the aging process.[6] The first rule is to "use it or lose it." The
human brain isn't like a calculator that you can plug in and leave
idle for a year and find working just as well when you return. It
must have constant use and regular input of sensory information.

Second, proper brain function is dependent on a balanced diet
with ample supplies of all the essential nutrients.

Third is exercise. Every organ of the body, including the

package of neural matter with which we think, benefits from physical activity.

Fourth is regular physical examinations and good health care. Untreated disease processes can affect us physically and mentally.

Finally, the fifth way to keep our brains healthy is by having an active social life. Being sick, isolated, and alone is a prescription for rapid mental decline.

Unfortunately, many older citizens are unable to implement these five suggestions for one reason or another. Some are alone and have no one to talk to. Others lack the resources for good medical care and healthy nutrition.

That's why those of us in the younger generation owe today's seniors our time and attention. They cared for us when we were frail and helpless. Now it's our time to return the favor.

Raising Boys Alone

ONE OF THE GREATEST CONTRIBUTIONS a single mother can make for a young son is to find him a mentor.

In her book, *Mothers and Sons,* the late Jean Lush talked about the challenges single mothers face in raising sons. The ages four to six are especially important and difficult. A boy at that age still loves his mother, but he feels the need to separate from her and gravitate toward a masculine image. If he has a father in the home, he'll usually want to spend more time with his dad apart from his mother and sisters.

But what advice can be given to a mother who is raising a son alone? First, she must understand that he has needs that she is not best equipped to meet. Her best option is to recruit a man who can act as a mentor to her son—one who can serve as a masculine role model. Of course, good mentors can be difficult to find. Single mothers should consider friends, relatives, or neighbors who can offer as little as an hour or two a month. In a pinch, a mature high schooler who likes kids could even be "rented" to play ball or go fishing with a boy in need.

Single women who belong to a Christian church should be able to find support for their boys among the male members of the community. Scripture commands people of faith to care for children without fathers. Isaiah 1:17 states, "Defend the cause of the fatherless, plead the case of the widow" (NIV). Jesus himself took boys and girls on his lap and said, "And whoever welcomes a little child like this in my name welcomes me" (Matt. 18:5, NIV). I believe it is our responsibility as Christian men to help single mothers with their difficult parenting tasks.

Certainly, single mothers have many demands on their time and energy, but the effort to find a mentor for their sons might be the most worthwhile contribution they can make.

The Magnificent Flying Machine

IS YOUR FAMILY SOARING ABOVE
the clouds right now—or are you weighed down by activities,
appointments, and acquisitions?

My friend Dennis Rainey tells the story of *Double Eagle
Two,* the first hot-air balloon to cross the Atlantic Ocean. The
men piloting the magnificent craft caught an air corridor that
carried them all the way across the Atlantic. But when they were
just off the coast of Ireland, they flew into heavy cloud cover, and
ice began to form on the balloon's outer shell. They lost altitude,
dropping from twenty thousand to ten thousand feet in a matter of
hours.

The crew did everything they could to save the balloon. They
threw over video cameras, food rations, and even a glider with
which they had planned to land. At about four thousand feet,
they transmitted their location, and then they threw the radio
overboard. Finally, at three thousand feet, they broke through

into sunlight. The ice came off in sheets, and the great balloon soared all the way into France.

Something similar to this scenario is repeated in homes today. The "family balloon" is encumbered by responsibilities, pressures, obligations, schedules, and entanglements. More and more activities are taken on board, causing the balloon to wobble and lose altitude. Many crash in the sea before they recognize the need to lighten the load.

There's a time to cut back, to simplify, to say no, and to spend more time at home. Then we can soar above the clouds, free and unencumbered by the things that would weigh us down.

The Attack of the Killer Hormones

WHAT IS THE PROCESS BY WHICH a happy, cooperative, twelve-year-old boy or girl suddenly turns into a sullen, depressed thirteen-year-old? It happens in almost every family.

There are two powerful forces that account for some of the adolescent behavior that drives parents crazy. The first is linked to the peer pressures that are common at that time. Much has been written about those influences. But there is a second, and I think more important, source of disruption of those years. It is related to the hormonal changes that not only transform the physical body, which we can see, but also revolutionize how kids think. For some (but not all) adolescents, human chemistry is in a state of imbalance for a few years, causing agitation, violent outbursts, depression, and flightiness. This upheaval can motivate a boy or girl to do things that make absolutely no sense to the adults who are watching anxiously on the sidelines. The hormonal firestorm operates much like premenstrual tension or menopause in women, destabilizing the self-concept and creating a sense of foreboding.

Parents often despair during the irrationality of this period. Everything they've tried to teach their sons and daughters seems to have misfired for a couple of years. Self-discipline, cleanliness, respect for authority, and common courtesy may give way to risk taking and all-around goofiness.

If that's where your child is today, I have good news for you. Better days are coming. That wacko kid will soon become a tower of strength and good judgment—if he doesn't do something destructive before his hormones settle down once more.

Challenge the Chief

HAVE YOU NOTICED THAT CHILDREN will occasionally disobey their parents for the express purpose of testing just how much they can get away with? This game, called challenge-the-chief, can be played with surprising skill, even by very young children.

One father told me recently of taking his three-year-old daughter to a basketball game. Naturally, this kid was interested in everything in the gymnasium except the game, so the father permitted her to roam free. But first he walked her down to the stripe painted on the gym floor, and he told her not to go past that line. No sooner had he returned to his seat than she went scurrying down to that forbidden territory and stopped at the border. Then she flashed a grin at her father and deliberately put one foot over the line. It was as if she were saying: "Whatcha gonna do about it?"

Virtually every parent the world over has been asked that

same question at one time or another. How it is answered is vitally important to the parent-child relationship. When a mom or dad ignores this kind of challenge, something changes in the mind of the child. For a particularly strong-willed boy or girl, that early test of parental leadership can grow into a full-blown case of rebellion during the troubled days of adolescence.

The ultimate paradox of childhood is that boys and girls want to be led by their parents, but they insist that their mothers and fathers earn the right to lead them. We should not miss the opportunity to do so.

The Real Cost of Divorce

DIVORCE CARRIES LIFELONG
negative implications for children.

It's now known that emotional development in children is
directly related to the presence of warm, nurturing, sustained, and
continuous interaction with *both* parents. Anything that interferes
with the vital relationship with either mother or father can have
lasting consequences for the child.

One landmark study[7] revealed that 90 percent of children
from divorced homes suffered from an acute sense of shock when
the separation occurred, including profound grieving and irrational
fears. Fifty percent reported feeling rejected and abandoned, and
indeed half of the fathers never came to see their children three
years after the divorce. One-third of the boys and girls feared
abandonment by the remaining parent, and 66 percent experienced
yearning for the absent parent with an intensity that researchers
described as overwhelming. Most significantly, 37 percent of the

children were even more unhappy and dissatisfied five years after the divorce than they had been at eighteen months. In other words, time did not heal their wounds.

That's the real meaning of divorce. It is certainly what I think about, with righteous indignation, when I see infidelity and marital deceit portrayed on television as some kind of exciting game for two. Some excitement. Some game.

Home Is Where Her Heart Is

ONE THING THAT MEN NEED TO understand is that, generally speaking, women tend to care more than men about the home and everything in it. It's certainly true in my house. Let me illustrate that point. A few years ago, my wife and I hired a plumber to install a gas-barbecue unit in the backyard, and then we left for the day. When we returned, we both observed that the device was mounted about eight inches too high.

Shirley and I stood looking at the appliance, and our reactions were quite different. I said, "Yeah, you're right. The plumber made a mistake. By the way, what are we having for dinner tonight?"

But Shirley reacted characteristically. She said, "I don't think I can stand that thing sticking up in the air like that."

I could have lived the rest of my life without thinking again about the height of the barbecue unit, but to Shirley it was a big deal. Why? Because to a man a home is a place where he can relax, kick off his shoes, and be himself. To a woman, especially a homemaker, the house is an extension of her personality. She expresses her individuality and her character through it. That's why husbands would be wise to recognize this differing perspective and accommodate the creative interests of their wives.

By the way, the plumber was summoned back to our house the next day and asked to fix his mistake. As the saying goes, "If Mama ain't happy, ain't nobody happy."

PREMARITAL COUNSELING CAN
make a great contribution to the stability of a future relationship.
My friend Dr. Archibald Hart, psychologist and author,
recommends at least six to eight counseling sessions before the bride
and groom meet at the altar. They are needed because those who
are engaged often have many expectations about marriage that are
never verbalized until after the knot has been tied. Conflict then
becomes inevitable when those differing assumptions collide.
Therefore, it is important to talk through these understandings
in the less antagonistic light of the courtship.

Dr. Hart often asks these kinds of questions to the couples
who consult with him:[8]

> "If I had never met the person you're planning to marry, and I had to
> rely on you to give me a description of who that individual is, what would
> you tell me?"

"If you could think of one thing that you would like to see your fiancé change, what would it be?"

"What are the five or six major goals that have been established for your first few years together?"

"What does your budget look like?"

"Have you planned how you're going to pay for the things you're going to buy beyond the honeymoon?"

Tough questions? You bet. But the couple that can't agree on these kinds of issues before they're married is certain to fight over them after the wedding. That's why I often recommend to the parents of engaged couples that they pay for premarital counseling as a wedding gift. It might be the most thoughtful gift you could provide.

The Window of Opportunity

THERE ARE SOME SKILLS THAT CAN be learned during the early childhood years that become very difficult to teach later on. For example, have you ever wondered why it's so easy for preschoolers to learn any language they hear? Russian, Chinese, Spanish, Hebrew—it really doesn't matter. Children can learn it perfectly without even a trace of an accent. Yet fifteen or twenty years later, most individuals will have a much harder time trying to make those same sounds.

Researchers now know why this is true. It's explained by a process known as "phoneme contraction." You see, the larynx of a young child assumes a shape necessary to make any sounds that he's learning to use at that time. It then solidifies or hardens in those positions, making it impossible or very difficult to make other sounds later in life. In other words, there's a window of opportunity when anything is possible linguistically, but it closes very quickly.

A child's attitude toward parental leadership is also like that. He or she passes through a brief period during toddlerhood and the preschool years when respect for authority and a certain sense of "awe" can be instilled. But that window closes very quickly. That's why it's so important to "shape the will" during the early years by balancing unconditional love with consistent firmness at home.

If parents miss that opportunity, the adolescent years can be bumpier than they need to be.

Preserving Your Family Heritage

THE LYRICS OF AN AFRICAN FOLK song say that when an old person dies, it's as if a library has burned down. It is true. There's a richness of family heritage in each person's life that will be lost if it isn't passed on to the next generation.

To preserve this heritage for our children we must tell them where we've been and how we got to this moment. Sharing about our faith, about our early family experiences, about the obstacles we overcame or the failures we suffered, can bring a family together and give it a sense of identity.

My great-grandmother (Nanny), who helped raise me when I was a boy, was nearly one hundred years old when she died. I loved for her to tell me tales about her early life on the frontier. A favorite story focused on the mountain lions that would prowl around her log cabin at night and attack the livestock. She could hear them growling and moving past her window as she lay in bed.

Nanny's father would try to chase the cats away with his rifle before they killed a pig or a goat. I would sit fascinated as this sweet lady described a world that had long vanished by the time I came on the scene. Her accounts of plains life helped open me to a love of history, a subject that still fascinates me to this day.

The stories of your past, of your childhood, of the courtship with your spouse, etc., can be treasures to your children. Unless you share those experiences with them, that part of their history will be gone forever. Take the time to make yesterday come alive for the kids in your family.

When Honesty Is Cruel

MOST MARRIAGE COUNSELORS emphasize communication as the foundation for a healthy relationship—nothing should be withheld from the marital partner. There is wisdom in that advice, provided it is applied with common sense.

It's true that couples who communicate openly have a much better chance of succeeding in marriage. But any good idea can be misused—at which point the effect becomes negative. For example, it's honest for a man to tell his wife that he hates her fat legs, or her varicose veins, or the way she cooks. It's honest for a woman to dump her anger on her husband and constantly berate him for his shortcomings and his failures. But honesty that does not have the best interest of the other person at heart is really a cruel form of selfishness. This is especially true when the other person can't help the characteristics that are being criticized.

Some couples, in their determination to share every thought

and opinion, systematically destroy the sweet spark of romance that once drew them together. No longer is there any sense of mystique in the relationship. They've unraveled the romantic allure that made them love one another in the first place.

I'm not suggesting that husbands and wives begin to deceive each other. I am recommending, however, that they leave something to be discovered along the way and occasionally let their anger and frustration cool down just a bit before pouring it on an unsuspecting partner in the name of honesty.

The bottom line? Let love be your guide.

Blank Slate or Complex Individual

DOES A NEWBORN BABY COME INTO
the world with a complex personality, or is that child a blank slate
on which experience will write?

In years past, behavioral scientists believed newborns had no
temperamental or emotional characteristics upon arrival from the
womb. Their little personalities were formed entirely by the
experiences that came their way in ensuing years. But most
parents knew better. Every mother of two or more children was
convinced that each of her infants had a different personality—
a different "feel"—from the very first time he or she was held.
Now, after years of research, numerous authorities in child
development acknowledge that those mothers were right.

One important study identified nine characteristics that varied
in babies—such as moodiness, level of activity, and responsiveness.
They also found that the differences from child to child tended to
persist into later life. It is my belief that babies differ in infinite

ways that define our humanness and our individuality. And how foolish of us to have thought otherwise. If every snowflake that falls has its own design and if every grain of sand at the seashore is unique, it makes no sense to suppose that children are stamped out as though they were manufactured by Henry Ford.

I'm not denying the importance of the environment and human experience in shaping who we are and how we think, but there can be no doubt that each person on earth is truly a one-of-a-kind creation from the earliest moments of life. There are no assembly lines in God's scheme of things.

The Only Cure for Bitterness

HAVE YOU NOTICED HOW DIFFICULT it is to forgive those who have wronged us? It's even harder when the offenders are our parents.

When we are young, our emotions are so intense that any wounds and injuries may stay with us for a lifetime. The pain is immeasurably worse when the one who wronged us was a parent. Perhaps a mother rejected us instead of providing the love we needed. Maybe an alcoholic father was sexually abusive in the midnight hours. Little victims of such horror may still be consumed by resentment and anger many decades later.

Psychologists and ministers now agree that there is only one cure for the cancer of bitterness. It is to forgive, which Dr. Archibald Hart defines as "giving up my right to hurt you for hurting me." [9] Only when we find the emotional maturity to release those who have wronged us, whether they have repented or not, will the wounds finally start to heal.

Jesus said it like this, "And when you stand praying, if you hold anything against anyone, forgive him, so that your Father in heaven may forgive you your sins" (Mark 11:25, NIV). Note that Jesus said nothing about who was right and who was wrong. Forgiveness, like love, must be unmerited and unconditional. Forgiveness begins the healing process.

TODAY'S EXTREME EMPHASIS
on physical attractiveness and body consciousness is harmful to
adults—and potentially life-threatening to children.

A study done at the University of California has shown that
80 percent of girls in the fourth grade have attempted to diet
because they see themselves as fat.[10] One elementary school girl
justified her dieting by saying she just wanted to be skinny so that
no one would tease her. How sad it is that children in this culture
have been taught to hate their bodies—to measure their worth by
comparison to a standard that they can never achieve. At a time
when they should be busy being kids, they're worried about how
much they weigh, how they look, and how they're seen by others.

For young girls, this insistence on being thin is magnified
by the cruelties of childhood. Dozens of studies now show that
overweight children are held in low regard by their peers, even at
an early age. According to one investigation, silhouettes of obese

children were described by six-year-olds as "lazy," "stupid," and "ugly."

This overemphasis on beauty does not occur in a vacuum, of course. Our children have caught our prejudices and our system of values. We, too, measure human worth largely on a scale of physical attractiveness. It's bad enough when adults evaluate each other that way. It's tragic when millions of children have already concluded that they're hopelessly flawed, even before life has gotten started.

EVERY SCHOOL HAS DOZENS OF boys and girls who are at the bottom of the social hierarchy. Some are physically unattractive, some are slow learners, and some are simply unable to make friends and find a comfortable place in the school environment.

The key question is: What should teachers do when they see one of these disrespected children being ridiculed and taunted by his peers? Some would say, "Kids will be kids. Stay out of the conflict, and let the children work out their differences for themselves." I disagree emphatically.

When a strong, loving teacher comes to the aid of the least respected child in the class, something dramatic occurs in the emotional climate of the room. Every child seems to utter an audible sigh of relief. The same thought bounces around in many little heads: *If that kid is safe from ridicule, then I must be safe, too.* By defending the least-popular child in the classroom, the teacher is demonstrating that she respects everyone and that she will fight for anyone who is being treated unfairly.

One of the values children cherish most is justice. They are, conversely, very uneasy in a world of injustice and abuse. Therefore, when we teach children kindness and respect for others by insisting on civility in our classrooms, we're laying a foundation for human kindness in the world of adulthood to come.

I say again to teachers: Defend the most defenseless child in your classroom.

SOMETIMES RAISING TEENAGERS
can be like sending an astronaut into space.

You may remember the very early space probes launched
from Cape Canaveral in the 1960s that created anxiety for the
safety of the astronaut. It was especially intense when the
spacecraft was reentering the earth's atmosphere. At the most
dangerous part of the journey, negative ions would accumulate
around the heat shield and interfere with radio contact for about
seven minutes. Finally, the reassuring voice of Chris Craft
would break in and say, "We've made contact with Colonel
Glenn again. Everything is A-OK."

In a very real sense, adolescence can be like that spacecraft.
After the training of childhood, a thirteen-year-old is blasted
into space with a flurry. Something like "negative ions" begins
to interfere with communication just as the adults want to be
assured of the child's safety. Why won't he talk to them?

Why has he or she disappeared behind a wall of silence? It is a terrifying time.

Fortunately, in a few years, the first scratchy signals will begin to come through again, and contact will be reestablished. The negative environment will gradually dissipate and the "splashdown" during the early twenties can be a wonderful reunion for both generations.

ONE OF THE MOST DIFFICULT
parenting responsibilities involves the orderly transfer of power to
our children. A common mistake is to grant autonomy before kids
are really ready to handle it. That can be a disaster for immature
and impulsive offspring. But it's just as dangerous to retain
parental power too long. Control will be torn from our grasp if
we refuse to surrender it voluntarily.

Consider, for example, how England treated her "children"
in the American colonies. The early settlers left the mother
country and grew to become rebellious "teenagers" who demanded
their freedom. Still, the British refused to release them, and much
unnecessary bloodshed resulted. England learned a valuable lesson
from that painful experience, however, and 171 years later she
granted a peaceful and orderly transfer of power to another
tempestuous offspring named India. Revolution was averted.

With regard to our children, the granting of self-determination must be matched stride-for-stride with the arrival of maturity, culminating with complete release during early adulthood. But the task isn't as easy as it sounds. The key is to chart a path between the two extremes of letting go too early and hanging on too long. Only great tact, wisdom, and prayer will help us determine the timing of that difficult decision.

ONE OF THE MOST DELICATE
aspects of raising a teenager is figuring out what's worth a show-
down and what isn't.

I remember talking to a waitress, a single mother in a restaurant
a few years ago. When she found out I was a psychologist, she
began telling me about her twelve-year-old daughter.

"We've fought tooth and nail this whole year," she said.
"It's been awful! We go at it every night—usually over the same
issue."

"What do you argue about?" I asked.

The mother spelled it out. "Well, she's still a little girl, but she
wants to shave her legs. I feel she's too young, but she gets so angry
she won't even talk to me. What do you think I should do?"

"Lady," I said, "go buy your daughter a razor."

That twelve-year-old girl would soon be paddling into a time
of life that would rock her canoe good and hard. Her mom, as a

single mother, would be trying desperately to keep this rebellious teenager from getting into drugs, alcohol, and premarital sex. Truly, there would be many ravenous alligators in her river within a year or two. In that setting it seemed unwise to make a big deal over what was essentially a nonissue.

I've seen other parents fight enormous battles over what were really inconsequential matters. It is a great mistake. I urge you not to damage your relationship with your kids over behavior that has no great moral or social significance. There'll be plenty of real issues that will require you to stand like a rock. Save your big guns for those crucial confrontations, and pretend not to notice that which is trivial.

WE LIVE UNDER A REPRESENTATIVE
form of government which Abraham Lincoln described as being
"of the people, by the people, and for the people." Unfortunately,
not enough of us take the time to let our representatives know how
we really feel about issues that concern us.

Letters and phone calls to our local officials, representatives,
and senators do make a difference, and these people certainly need
to hear from us. Let me offer a few ideas that may help in making
your letter the most effective it can be. First, be brief, and restrict
each letter to one subject or one piece of legislation. This makes is
easier for the person you're writing to to respond and for their
staff to organize correspondence. If the letter is about a specific
bill, identify it by name and number. Second, make your letter
personal. Form letters and postcards do have a place, but
personal letters get more attention. Describe how the proposed
bill or course of action would affect you or your family or your

community. Give the essential background information as well. And third, remember that elected officials receive thousands of letters of complaint and very few positive responses.

If a public official says or does something that you like, respond with a quick note of appreciation, and by all means, remember that democracy works best when the people make their wants and wishes known.

IT IS WELL KNOWN THAT A DIFFICULT childhood leaves some people wounded and disadvantaged for the rest of their lives. But for others, early hardships actually fuel great achievement and success. The difference appears to be a function of individual temperaments and resourcefulness.

In a classic study called *Cradles of Eminence,* Victor and Mildred Goertzel investigated the home backgrounds of three hundred highly successful people. The researchers sought to identify the early experiences that may have contributed to remarkable achievement. All of the subjects were well known for their accomplishments; they included Einstein, Freud, Churchill, and many others.[11]

The backgrounds of these people proved very interesting. Three-fourths of them came from troubled childhoods, enduring poverty, broken homes, or parental abuse. One-fourth had physical handicaps. Most of those who became writers and playwrights had watched their own parents embroiled in psychological dramas of one sort or another. The researchers concluded that the need to compensate for disadvantages was a major factor in the drive toward personal achievement.

The application to your own family should be obvious. If your child has gone through a traumatic experience or is physically disadvantaged, don't give up hope. Help identify his or her strengths and natural abilities that can be used to overcome the handicap.

Whether your child's challenges ultimately weaken or strengthen him or her may be influenced by the way you respond to the crisis. The problem that seems so formidable today may become the inspiration for greatness tomorrow.

Using Reinforcement and Extinction

IT'S A WELL-KNOWN FACT THAT
behavior that is not rewarded will eventually disappear. This
process is called "extinction," and it can be a very useful tool for
parents and teachers.

Have you ever wondered, for example, why so many young
children develop a tendency to whine when they speak to their
parents? Simply stated: Children whine because whining works.
Mom and Dad are too busy and too preoccupied to respond to a
normal voice. But they react immediately when their kids irritate
them with a grating, unpleasant sound. What the parents are
doing is rewarding (or "reinforcing") the whining response and
extinguishing the more desirable behavior.

How can this process be reversed? Well, you might try
saying, "Johnny, did you know I have very funny ears? They
can't hear a whining voice. I can only hear a pleasant voice."
Then proceed to ignore anything said in an irritating tone, but

respond immediately when the normal voice is used. In this way, reward and extinction instantly become powerful tools for parents who understand properly how they work.

Remember this guiding principle: Behavior that produces desirable results will recur, and behavior that fails in the eyes of the child will tend to go away. It's as simple as that.

THERE ARE SOME FACTS OF NATURE that never cease to astound me. For instance, did you know that before it snows, fir trees in northern regions actually retract their branches so that the weight of the snow they'll have to bear will be reduced? This withdrawal response is programmed into every branch, even in those smaller than a little finger. The Creator has enabled the tree to anticipate the problem before it occurs, thereby reducing the risks that might accompany a snowy winter.

Perhaps we can do something similar within our own marriages. You will not be able to avoid problems and crises in marriage, but you can anticipate them and prepare for their arrival. Most of the stress points in families are common to others and are therefore predictable.

One of my good friends spent a considerable amount of time with his wife preparing for the moment when their grown kids would move out of the house. They talked often about the empty nest and discussed ways their friends had coped with it. They read books about that phase of life and applied what they had heard to themselves. As a result, their transition to the empty nest was smooth and uneventful.

Into every marriage, a little snow will fall. Blizzards will blow, and storms will howl. But an effort to anticipate these difficult times will help you and your mate stand up under the weight of the winter storm.

WOULDN'T IT BE INTERESTING TO
hold a national convention sometime, bringing together all the
mothers who have experienced the particular traumas of raising
one or more toddlers?

If that occurred, we'd hear some amazingly similar stories.
Hasn't every mother opened a bedroom door unexpectedly to find
her little tiger covered with lipstick from the top of her pink head
to the soles of her sneakers? On the wall is her own artistic
creation with a red handprint right in the center, and throughout
the room is the aroma of perfume with which she has just anointed
her baby brother.

What should you do if you find yourself in this situation?
Sure, there's a mess to be cleaned up, but I hope you would find
humor in the experience. And why not? Laughter can be the key
to survival during the stresses of raising kids. If you can see the
delightful side of your assignment, you can also deal with the

difficult side. Almost every day I hear from mothers who have learned to use the ballast of humor to keep their boats afloat. They know that these child-rearing years will be but a dim memory in a brief moment or two.

As the father of two grown children, let me urge the parents of young children to hug 'em while you can. They'll be grown before you know it.

Combating "Soul Hunger"

WOMEN WHO FEEL ISOLATED AND lonely often look to their husbands to satisfy what has been called their "soul hunger." It is a role men have never handled very well. I doubt if farmers came in from the fields one hundred years ago to have heart-to-heart talks with their wives.

What *has* changed in that time is the relationship between women. A century ago, great support and camaraderie existed between wives and mothers. They cooked together, went to church together, and grew old together. And when a baby was born, aunts, grandmothers, and neighbors were there to show the new mother how to diaper, feed, and discipline.

Today, however, the extended family has all but disappeared, depriving women of that traditional source of support. Furthermore, American families move every three or four years, preventing long-term friendships from developing.

It's also important for women to understand that some of their needs simply can't be met by men.

In the classic book, *Anne of Green Gables* by Lucy M. Montgomery, there's a wonderful moment when the teenage Anne says, "A bosom friend—an intimate friend, you know—a really kindred spirit to whom I can confide my inmost soul. I've dreamed of meeting her all my life." She expresses a longing that is common to women, but not so typical in men. It's the need for intimate friendship. I think this is a key to understanding the incidence of depression common among many women today.

To combat this sense of isolation, it is extremely important for women to maintain a network of friends through exercise classes, group hobbies, church activities, or bicycle clubs. The interchange between them may sound like casual talk, but the bonding that occurs there makes life a lot more satisfying.

The Classic Underachiever

HAVE YOU EVER SEEN THOSE BART Simpson T-shirts around? You know, the ones that say "Underachiever—And Proud of It" ? In real life, however, most underachievers are not really all that happy about their lack of performance.

The underachiever is a child who has the ability to do required schoolwork but does not have the self-discipline to perform. He slowly drives his mother, father, and teachers crazy as assignment after assignment hits the floor.

So what's a parent to do? Anger is the typical response, but it is most ineffective. Instead, I would make three recommendations that can reach some kids. First, since most underachievers are terribly disorganized, help establish a system for studying. Turn off the television set, and make sure the proper investment in homework is made. Second, stay in close contact with his teachers and know what's going on in school. I promise you that your underachieving son or daughter will *not* keep you so informed. And third, seek tutorial assistance to provide the one-on-one help that may make the difference.

Having offered that advice, however, let me speak now out of the other side of my mouth. There are some hard-core underachievers who seem determined to fail in school. For them no amount of pushing and shoving will get them motivated. In those cases I recommend that you go with the flow and accept the child just as he is. Not every youngster can be squeezed into the same mold, and it's a wise parent who knows when to race the engine and when to let it idle.

If there were a simple, single solution to the pervasive problem of underachievement, I'd put it in a bottle and sell it by the millions. It sure couldn't be any less helpful than those Bart Simpson T-shirts.

Who's at Fault When Kids Go Bad?

WHOSE FAULT IS IT WHEN A TEENAGER gets into trouble? Who gets the blame when he or she skips school or sprays graffiti on a bridge or begins to experiment with drugs? Whom do we accuse?

In the eyes of culture, parents are inevitably responsible for the misbehavior of their teenagers, and certainly, many deserve that criticism. Some are alcoholics or child abusers, or they have otherwise damaged their kids through their own blunders. But it's time we admitted that the sons and daughters of some very loving, caring parents can go wrong, too.

Only in this century have we blamed all misbehavior of teenagers on their parents. In years past, if a kid went bad, he was a bad kid. Now it's inevitably the fault of his dear old mom and dad, who must have bungled his childhood in some way. Well, maybe, and maybe not. Adolescents are old enough to make irresponsible choices of their own, and some do stupid things despite the love and care they receive at home.

I would not seek to exonerate parents who have shortchanged their kids and treated them badly. But someone should speak on behalf of those good-as-gold moms and dads who did the best they could for their rebellious children. They deserve a pat on the back, not a slap in the face.

Mistaken Identity

JAIME ESCALANTE, THE GARFIELD High School teacher on whom the movie *Stand and Deliver* was based, once told me this story about a fellow teacher. During his first year in the classroom, he had two students named Johnny. One was a happy child, an excellent student, a fine citizen. The other Johnny spent much of his time goofing off and making a nuisance of himself.

When the PTA held its first meeting of the year, a mother came up to this teacher and asked, "How's my son, Johnny, getting along?" He assumed she was the mom of the better student and replied, "I can't tell you how much I enjoy him. I'm so glad he's in my class."

The next day the problem child came to the teacher and said, "My mom told me what you said about me last night. I haven't ever had a teacher who wanted me in his class."

That day he completed his assignments and brought in his

completed homework the next morning. A few weeks later, the "problem" Johnny had become one of this teacher's hardest working students—and one of his best friends. This misbehaving child's life was turned around all because he was mistakenly identified as a good student.

Not every lazy or underachieving boy or girl could be motivated by a simple compliment from a teacher, of course, but there is a principle here that applies to all kids: It's better to make a child stretch to reach your high opinion than stoop to match your disrespect.

A FEW YEARS AGO, MY TEENAGE son and I got up one morning and situated ourselves in a deer blind before the break of day. About twenty yards away from us was a feeder that operated on a timer. At 7:00 A.M., it automatically dropped kernels of corn into a pan below. Ryan and I huddled together in the blind, talking softly about whatever came to mind. Then through the fog, we saw a beautiful doe emerge. She came silently into the clearing and moved toward the feeder. We had no intention of shooting her, of course, but it was fun to watch this beautiful animal from close range. The doe ate a quick breakfast and fled.

I whispered to Ryan, "There's something valuable to be learned from what we've just seen. Whenever you come upon a free supply of high-quality corn unexpectedly provided right there in the middle of the forest, be careful. The people who put it there are probably sitting nearby just waiting to take a shot at you."

Ryan may not always remember that advice, but I will. It isn't often that a father says something that he considers to be profound to his teenage son. One thing is certain: This interchange and the other ideas that we shared on that day would not have occurred at home. Opportunities for that kind of communication have to be created. Those teachable moments occur when you have set aside time to be with people you love, especially your children. Preserve them at all cost.

IT'S NOT THE QUANTITY OF TIME that you spend with your children, it's the quality that counts. Or is it?

Maybe you've heard the argument that it doesn't matter how little time you spend with your children as long as your few moments together are especially meaningful. But the logic of that concept seems suspect to me. The question is, why do we have to choose between the virtues of quantity versus quality? We won't accept that forced choice in any other area of our lives. So why is it only relevant to our children?

Let me illustrate my point. Let's suppose you've looked forward all day to eating at one of the finest restaurants in town. The waiter brings you a menu, and you order the most expensive steak in the house. But when the meal arrives, you see a tiny piece of meat about one inch square in the center of the plate. When you complain about the size of the steak, the waiter says,

"Sir, I recognize that the portion is small, but that's the finest corn-fed beef money can buy. You'll never find a better bite of meat than we've served you tonight. As to the portion, I hope you understand that it's not the quantity that matters, it's the quality that counts."

You would object, and for good reason. Why? Because both quality and quantity are important in many areas of our lives, including how we relate to children. They need our time and the best we have to give them.

My concern is that the quantity versus quality argument might be a poorly disguised rationalization for giving our children—neither.

SIBLING RIVALRY WAS RESPONSIBLE for the first murder on record when Cain killed Abel, and it's been occurring at a furious pace ever since.

While conflict between brothers and sisters occurs in virtually every family, it is possible to lessen the antagonism and create a more family-friendly atmosphere in the home. The key is for parents to enforce a reasonable set of boundaries between warring factions.

Robert Frost said, "Good fences make good neighbors." I agree. People get along better when there are reasonable boundaries between them and when law and order are evident. Suppose I lived in a frontier town where there were no police officers, no courts, and no city ordinances. My neighbor and I would be much more likely to fuss with one another than in a modern society where the laws are known and a mechanism exists for their enforcement.

And so it is with children in a family. Everyone gets along better when there are reasonable rules that are enforced with fairness. Otherwise, chaos reigns. When the older child can make life miserable for a younger boy or girl or when the younger can break the toys and mess up the things of his big brother or sister, hatred is more likely to be fomented. It is a consequence of the lawless environment in which they live.

That's why I strongly recommend that parents set up reasonable rules for harmonious living at home and then enforce them with the full weight of their authority. Only then can children live peacefully with their little rivals down the hall.

Why We Study

IT'S BEEN SAID THAT WE FORGET more than 80 percent of what we learn. The obvious question is, "Why, then, should we go to the trouble of learning at all?"

When you consider the cost of getting an education, it seems appropriate that we justify all that effort going into examinations, textbooks, homework, and countless hours spent in boring classrooms. Is education really worth what we invest in it?

In fact, it is. There are many valid reasons for learning, even if forgetting will take its usual toll. First, maybe the most important function of the learning process is the self-discipline and self-control that it fosters. Good students learn to follow directions, carry out assignments, and channel their mental faculties. Second, even if the facts and concepts can't be recalled, the individual knows they exist and where to find them. He or she can retrieve the information if needed. Third, old learning makes new learning easier. Each mental exercise gives us more associative cues with which to link future ideas and concepts, and we are changed for having been through the process of learning. Fourth, we don't really forget everything that is beyond the reach of our memories. The information is stored in the brain and will return to consciousness when properly stimulated. And fifth, we are shaped by the influence of intelligent and charismatic people who teach us.

I wish there were an easier, more efficient process for shaping human minds than the slow and painful experience of education. But until a "learning pill" is developed, the old-fashioned approach will have to do.

Mutual Admiration

OUR SENSE OF SELF-RESPECT IS often based on the reactions, positive or negative, of those around us. That is especially true in the intimate context of marriage.

Dr. Paul Brand was a flight surgeon during World War II. He tells in one of his books of a fine young man named Peter Foster, who was a Royal Air Force pilot. Foster flew a Hurricane, which was a fighter with a design flaw: The single-propeller engine was mounted in the front, and the fuel lines ran past the cockpit. In a direct hit, the pilot would instantly be engulfed in flames before he could eject. The consequences were often tragic.

Some RAF pilots caught in that inferno would undergo ten or twenty surgeries to reconstruct their faces. Peter Foster was one of those downed pilots whose face was burned beyond recognition. But Foster had the support of his family and the love of his fiancée. She assured him that nothing had changed except a few millimeters of skin. Two years later they were married.

Foster said of his wife, "She became my mirror. She gave me a new image of myself. When I look at her, she gives me a warm, loving smile that tells me I'm OK."

That's the way marriage ought to work, even when disfigurement has not occurred. It should be a mutual-admiration society that builds the self-esteem of both partners and overlooks a million flaws that could otherwise be destructive. There's a word for that kind of commitment: We call it *love*.

Defending "the Line of Respect"

ONE OF THE BEST WAYS TO KEEP
a marriage healthy is to maintain a system of mutual accountability
within the context of love. This is done by protecting what I call
"the line of respect" in a marital relationship. Let me illustrate.

Suppose I work in my office two hours longer than usual on
a particular night, knowing that my wife, Shirley, is at home
preparing a very special candlelight dinner. If I don't call to let
her know I'll be late, you can bet that I'm going to hear about it
when I get home. Shirley would see my behavior as insulting—
and she'd be right. So she'd say, in effect, "Jim, what you did
was selfish, and I can't let it pass." In those few words, and
probably a few more, she would have spoken her mind in love
and held me accountable for my disrespect. Then we would move
on together.

In a healthy marriage, some things are worth defending, and
mutual respect is at the top of the list. This doesn't mean you

should nag, insult, publicly embarrass your mate, or point out insignificant indiscretions that should be overlooked. But a workable system of "checks and balances" can keep your marriage on course when issues of respect are at stake.

This kind of mutual accountability is the best way I know to avoid an unexpected explosion when stored resentment and anger reach a critical mass.

Maximizing Your Child's Potential

ACCORDING TO A TEN-YEAR STUDY conducted by Dr. Burton White and a team of researchers at Harvard University, there are six factors that are related to the eventual intellectual capacity of a child:

1. The most critical period for the child's mental development is between eight and eighteen months of age.
2. The mother is the most important person in the child's environment.
3. The amount of "live" language directed to the child between twelve and fifteen months is absolutely crucial.
4. Those children who are given free access to living areas of their homes progressed much faster than those whose movements are restricted.
5. The nuclear family is the most important educational delivery system.
6. The best parents are those who excel at three key functions: They are also superb designers and organizers of their children's environments; they permit their children to interrupt them for brief thirty-second episodes, during which personal comfort and information are exchanged; finally, they are firm disciplinarians while simultaneously showing great affection for their children.[12]

In other words, this ten-year investigation conducted by learned researchers revealed precisely what most mothers have always known they should do: Love their kids, talk to them, treat them with respect, expose them to interesting things, organize their time, discipline them fairly, and raise them in strong and stable families. It is a time-honored recipe for producing bright (and happy) children.

Go with the Flow

SOME KIDS APPEAR TO BE BORN TO lead, and others seem to be made to follow. And that fact can be a cause of concern for parents at times.

One mother told me that her compliant, easygoing child was being picked on and beat up every day in nursery school. She urged him to defend himself, but it contradicted his very nature to even think about standing up to the bullies. Finally, his frustration became so great that he decided to heed his mother's advice. As they drove to school one day he said, "Mom, if those kids pick on me again today . . . I'm . . . I'm . . . I'm going to beat them up—slightly!"

How does a kid beat up someone slightly? I don't know, but it made perfect sense to this compliant lad.

Parents sometimes worry about this kind of easygoing, passive child—especially if the child is a boy. Followers in this society are sometimes less respected than aggressive leaders, and they can be seen as wimpy or spineless. And yet, the beauty of the human personality is seen in its marvelous complexity. There is a place for the wonderful variety of personalities that find expression in a child. After all, if two people are identical in temperament and point of view, it's obvious that one of them is unnecessary.

My advice to parents is to accept, appreciate, and cultivate the personality with which your little child is born. He need not fit a preconceived mold. That youngster is, thankfully, one of a kind.

Children and Materialism

IT'S NOT EASY TO SAY NO TO children, especially in an affluent and permissive society. Toy companies are spending millions of dollars on advertising aimed at children—not their parents. They know boys and girls are the very best customers. But by giving in to this pressure, parents may actually deprive their children of pleasure. Here's why.

Pleasure occurs when an intense need is met. A glass of water is worth more than gold to a person who's dying of thirst, but it's worthless to the person who doesn't need it. That principle applies directly to children. If you never allow a boy or girl to desire something, he or she will not fully enjoy the pleasure of receiving it. If you give him a tricycle before he can walk, and a bike before he can ride, and a car before he can drive, and a diamond ring before he knows the value of money, you may actually have deprived him of the satisfaction he could have received from that possession.

How unfortunate is the child who never has the opportunity to long for something, to dream about that prize by day, and to plot for it by night, perhaps even to get desperate enough to work for it.

Excessive materialism is not only harmful to children—but it deprives them of pleasure, too.

YOU TALK AND TALK, BUT YOUR partner just doesn't seem to comprehend. Have you ever had that experience? Well, maybe it's time you tried a new form of communication.

One very effective way to express your feelings is to paint a word picture. My good friends Gary Smalley and John Trent described this technique in their book *The Language of Love.* They told of a woman who was feeling frustrated because her husband would come home from work and clam up. He had nothing to say all evening. Finally, his wife told him a story about a man who went to breakfast with some friends. He ate a big meal, and then he gathered up some crumbs and put them in a bag. Then he went to lunch with some business associates and ate a big steak. Again, he put a few of the crumbs in a bag to take home. When he came home that night, he handed his wife the little bag of leftovers. The woman told her husband, "That's what you are doing to me. All day the children and I wait to talk with you when you get home. But you don't share yourself with us. After being gone all day, you hand us a doggie bag and turn on the television set." The husband said hearing it put this way was like being hit with a two-by-four. He apologized and began to work on opening himself to his wife and family.

Word pictures. They are far more effective than a tornado of hostile words.

HAVE YOU NOTICED THAT FAMILY
members can become world-class experts at manipulating one
another?

Deep within the human spirit is the desire for raw power. We
want to run our own lives and everyone else's, if we can. There
are dozens of techniques that people commonly use to control those
around them. Among them are

- Emotional blackmail: "Do what I want or I'll get very angry and go all
  to pieces."
- The guilt trip: "How could you do this to me after I've done so much for
  you?"
- The eternal illness: "Don't upset me. Can't you see I'm sick?"
- Help from beyond the grave: "Your dear father would've agreed with me."
- Divine revelation: "God told me you should do what I want."
- The humiliation: "Do what I want or I'll embarrass you at home and
  abroad."

These are powerful tools that are used every day in getting others to dance to a different tune. Not only are adults good at using them, but teenagers can be masters of manipulation. Their techniques include teenage terror: "Leave me alone or I'll pull a stupid adolescent stunt (suicide, alcohol, drugs, and so on)," or fertile follies: "Do what I want or I'll present you with a baby." That threat unravels the nerves of every adult.

Manipulation is a game any number can play—right in the privacy of your own home. But those who engage in it pay a dear price in conflict, hostility, and resentment.

Protecting the Compliant Child

WE'VE TALKED BEFORE ABOUT children whose temperaments are naturally compliant, compared with those who are born with tough, assertive personalities. For some reason, every parent with two or more children is probably blessed with at least one of each.

When one child is a stick of dynamite and the other is an all-star sweetheart, the cooperative, gentle individual can easily be taken for granted. If there's an unpleasant job to be done, she may be expected to do it because Mom and Dad just don't have the energy to fight with the tiger. When it is necessary for one child to sacrifice or do without, there's a tendency to pick the one who won't complain as loudly. Under these circumstances, the compliant child comes out on the short end of the stick.

The consequences of such inequity should be obvious. The responsible child often becomes angry over time. She has a sense of powerlessness and resentment that simmers below the surface.

He's like the older brother in the parable of the Prodigal Son told by Jesus. He didn't rebel against his father, but he resented the attention given to his irresponsible brother. That's a typical response. I strongly recommend that parents seek to balance the scales in dealing with the compliant child. Make sure he gets his fair share of parental attention. Help him find ways to cope with his overbearing sibling. And, within reason, give him the right to make his own decisions.

There's nothing simple about raising kids. Even the "easiest" of them need our very best effort.

New Rules to the Courtship Game

THERE WAS A TIME WHEN YOUNG girls were taught to be reserved—to keep a tight rein on their impulses—especially when it came to matters of the heart. They would never have asked a boy for a date, or even have made the first telephone call. But much of that has changed, I believe, for the worse.

The sexual revolution of the past twenty years has had a dramatic effect on the way the courtship game is played. Boys have traditionally been the initiators, and girls were once quite content to be the responders. But what we're seeing now is a new sexual aggressiveness among females that has many parents worried.

Some girls are so bold sexually and have such a hard-charging approach that males are intimidated and anxious to escape that firepower. The male ego is constructed in such a way that many men are uncomfortable if not in pursuit. Even in this day when the old restrictions and taboos for women have fallen away,

I believe it's still appropriate for parents to teach their girls a certain reserve, a certain self-respect when it comes to romantic relationships. This is especially true during the awkward experiences of early adolescence.

It may be difficult for a girl to pull in her horns a bit, but she'll be more successful and less vulnerable by attracting the object of her affection, rather than trying to run him down.

SOME TEENAGERS CAN'T WAIT TO get out of the house and on their own. Others don't go quite as willingly. How do you get your grown child to move on when the time has come?

Sometimes independence eludes young adults not because parents withhold it but because sons and daughters refuse to accept it. They have no intention of growing up, and why should they? The nest is just too comfortable at home. Food is prepared. Clothes are laundered, and bills are paid. There's no incentive to face the cold world of reality, and they are determined not to budge. Some even refuse to work. I know it's difficult to dislodge a homebound son or daughter. They're like furry little puppies who hang around the back door waiting for a saucer of warm milk. But to let them stay year after year, especially if they're not pursuing career goals, is to cultivate irresponsibility and dependency. That's not love, even though it may feel like it. There comes the time when you must gently but forthrightly hand the reins over to your child and force him to stand on his own. You might even have to help him pack.

Learning to Fight Fair

SINCE CONFLICT EXISTS IN EVERY romantic relationship, learning to fight fair just might be the most important lesson a couple can master.

The first obligation is to understand the difference between healthy and unhealthy combat in marriage. In an unstable marriage, hostility is aimed at the partner's soft underbelly with comments like "You never do anything right!" and "Why did I marry you in the first place?" and "You're getting more like your mother every day!" These offensive remarks strike at the very heart of the mate's self-worth.

Healthy conflict, by contrast, remains focused on the issues that cause disagreement. For example: "It upsets me when you don't tell me you're going to be late for dinner" or "I was embarrassed when you made me look foolish at the party last night." Can you hear the difference?

Even though the two approaches may be equally contentious,

the first assaults the dignity of the partner while the second addresses the source of conflict. When couples learn this important distinction, they can work through their disagreements without wounding and insulting each other.

Basic civility is one of the building blocks of lifelong marriage.

Maintaining a Reserve Army

A GOOD MILITARY GENERAL WILL never commit all of his soldiers to the battlefield at the same time. He keeps a reserve force to relieve exhausted soldiers when they stagger back from the front lines. Parents of teenagers would do well to follow the same strategy. Let me explain.

It is common today for mothers of preschoolers to believe that the heavy demands of raising children will diminish once her kids reach school age. Then, she thinks, she can accept a heavier workload and other activities without sacrificing the needs of her children. It is my belief that the teenage years often generate more pressure and make greater demands on parents than when their kids are small. Besides the common rebellion of those years, there's the chauffeuring, the supervising, the cooking and cleaning, the noise and chaos that surround an ambitious teenager. Someone in the family must be available to respond to these challenges and the other stresses associated with adolescence.

It's a wise parent, then, who takes care not to exhaust himself or herself when so much is going on at home. A reservoir of energy is needed to deal with the unexpected and the difficult. To the degree possible, keep the family schedule simple, get plenty of rest, eat nutritious meals, and prepare to deal competently with the challenges of those years.

This is why I believe, though many will disagree, that it is as important for mothers of teenagers to be at home as it is for those raising preschoolers. That's the best way to maintain a reserve army when it's needed most.

Compensatory Skills

IT'S NOT EASY GETTING THROUGH adolescence today, and the effective parent must learn early how to brace his or her kids before those turbulent years arrive.

Perhaps the most painful aspect of growing up is related to the assault on self-esteem that is almost universal in today's teen society. Young people typically feel like fools and failures before they've even had a chance to get started in life. So how can parents prepare their younger children for the teenage years to come? Is there any way to make that passage to adulthood any easier and safer?

Well, one important approach is to teach boys and girls valuable skills with which to provide a centerpiece in their self-identity in years to come. They can benefit from learning about basketball, tennis, electronics, art, music, or even raising rabbits for fun and profit. It's not so much what you teach your child. The key is that he or she learn something with which to compensate when the whole world seems to be saying, "Who are you, and what is your significance as a human being?"

The teenager who has no answer to those questions is left unprotected at a very vulnerable time of life. Developing and honing skills with which to compensate may be one of the most valuable contributions parents can make during the elementary school years. It may even be worth requiring your carefree kid to take lessons, practice, compete, and learn something he or she will not fully appreciate for a few more years.

The Greatest Danger

I'M OFTEN ASKED WHAT I PERCEIVE to be the greatest threat to families today. I could talk, in response, about alcoholism, drug abuse, infidelity, and the other common causes of divorce. But there is another curse that accounts for more family breakups than the others combined. It is the simple matter of overcommitment and the tyranny of the urgent.

Husbands and wives who fill their lives with never-ending volumes of work are too exhausted to take walks together, to share their deeper feelings, to understand and meet each other's needs. They're even too worn out to have a meaningful sexual relationship, because fatigue is a destroyer of desire.

This breathless pace predominates in millions of households, leaving every member of the family frazzled and irritable. Husbands are moonlighting to bring home more money. Wives are on their own busy career track. Children are often ignored, and life goes speeding by in a deadly routine. Even some grandparents are too busy to keep the grandkids. I see this kind of overcommitment as the quickest route to the destruction of the family. And there simply must be a better way.

Some friends of mine recently sold their house and moved into a smaller and less expensive place just so they could lower their payments and reduce the hours required in the workplace. That kind of downward mobility is almost unheard of today—it's almost un-American. But when we reach the end of our lives and we look back on the things that mattered most, those precious relationships with people we love will rank at the top of the list.

If friends and family will be a treasure to us then, why not live like we believe it today? That may be the best advice I have ever given anyone—and the most difficult to implement.

IF CONFIDENCE IS SOMETHING WE value for our sons and daughters, maybe it would be helpful to assist them in achieving it.

Today it seems like every teenager has to come along and bump his or her head on the same ol' rock, experiencing those terrible feelings of inadequacy and inferiority. To help kids minimize that experience, I've found it beneficial to talk to them about confidence long before adolescence has arrived.

For example, when your child meets another boy or girl who's very shy, you might say afterward, "Did you notice that Pam didn't look at anyone when she spoke? Why do you suppose she seemed so embarrassed and uncomfortable? Do you think it's because she doesn't have much confidence in herself?"

Then in the period immediately before puberty, make it known that the teen years are often accompanied by a massive assault on self-worth, where everybody seems to feel ugly and unintelligent and useless. But also explain that this is a temporary experience, like going through a tunnel from which you will inevitably emerge. It would also be wise in this twilight of childhood to discuss the sexual awakening that's about to occur, including how the body will change and how to use this new experience responsibly and morally. To not do so is to leave the child to cope alone with the terrors of menstruation or other physical transformations.

So much can be done to prepare kids for the coming crises in adolescence if we'll give a little thought to the task.

Engine and Caboose

DID YOU HEAR THE ONE ABOUT THE wedding ceremony where the minister said, "Do you take this woman for better or for worse? For richer or for poorer? In sickness and in health?" And the groom said, "Yes, no, yes, no, no, yes."

Of course, we'd all like to sign up for the better, richer, and healthier parts when we get married and forget all that other stuff. But that's not the way marriage works because that's not the way life works.

I heard of another wedding ceremony, this one real, during which the bride and groom pledged to stay married as long as they continued to love each other. Well, I hope they both know good divorce attorneys, because they're going to need them. Relationships based on feelings are necessarily ephemeral and transitory. The only real stability in marriage is produced by firm commitments that hold two people steady when emotions are fluctuating wildly. Without this determination to cement human relationships, they are destined to disintegrate.

Can you imagine a parent saying to the child, "I'll care for you for as long as I shall love you" ? That would hardly portend stability and well-being for the child. Nor does a wishy-washy expression of love hold much promise for the future of a marriage.

Emotion might be thought of as the caboose on a train. A committed will is the engine that pulls the relationship through all the ups and downs of everyday living.

Helping a Single Mom

MANY YEARS AGO, MY WIFE, Shirley, was working around the house one morning when a knock came at the front door. When she opened it, there stood a young woman in her late teens who called herself Sally.

"I'm selling brushes," she said, "and I wonder if you'd like to buy any."

Well, my wife told her she wasn't interested in buying anything that day, and Sally said, "I know. No one else is, either." And with that, she began to cry.

Shirley invited Sally to come in for a cup of coffee, and she asked her to share her story. She turned out to be an unmarried mother who was struggling mightily to support her two-year-old son. That night, we went to her shabby little apartment above a garage to see how we could help this mother and her toddler. When we opened the cupboards, there was nothing there for them to eat, and I mean nothing. That night, they both dined on a can of SpaghettiOs. We took her to the market, and we did what we could to help get her on her feet.

Sally is obviously not the only single mother out there who is desperately trying to survive in a very hostile world. All of these mothers could use a little kindness—from baby-sitting to providing a meal to repairing the washing machine or even to just showing a little thoughtfulness.

Raising kids all alone is the toughest job in the universe. Do you suppose there's someone in your neighborhood who is going down for the third time? How about giving her a helping hand? Not only will it bring encouragement to the mother, but one or more children will bless you, as well.

It's All Hard Work

WHEN I HEAR SOMEONE COMMENT that being a mother and homemaker is boring, I have a simple response: You could be right!

The truth is, almost any occupation you can name—from a telephone operator to a medical pathologist to an attorney or a dentist—involves long hours of tedious activity. Few of us enjoy heart-thumping excitement each moment of our professional lives. I once stayed in a hotel right next to the room of a famous cellist who was performing in a classical concert that evening. I could hear him through the walls as he practiced hour after hour. He didn't play beautiful symphonic renditions; he repeated scales and runs and exercises, over and over and over. Believe me! This practice began early in the morning and continued until the time of his concert. As he strolled onto the stage that night, I'm sure many in the audience thought to themselves, *What a glamorous life!* Some glamour! I happen to know he spent the entire day in his lonely hotel room in the company of his cello.

No, I doubt if the job of being a mother and homemaker is more boring than most other jobs, particularly if a woman refuses to be isolated from adult contact. But regarding the importance of the assignment, no job can compete with the satisfaction of shaping and molding and guiding a new human being.

Preparing for College

IF YOUR SON OR DAUGHTER IS college bound, you've probably spent hours filling out forms, discussing loans, and deciding which colleges to visit. But there are a few more ways you can help prepare for this first experience away from home.

For starters, author Joan Wester Anderson suggests that you make sure that your teen has the basic skills necessary to survive dorm life. Can he or she operate a washer and dryer, stick to a budget, handle a checkbook, get along with roommates, and manage his or her time wisely?

It's important as well to prepare your son or daughter for the negative aspects of campus life. Too often, adults present a rosy portrait of college as "the best years of life," which creates unrealistic expectations that lead to disappointment. Remind your child that homesickness is to be expected and that he or she can call home collect anytime, just to chat.

It's helpful to talk about those matters beforehand. During the first semester away, letters and treats from home can ease the pain of separation anxiety. And be enthusiastic when that son or daughter returns for visits. If she feels like an intruder, she just might decide to visit someone else's home for future vacations.

Going away to college is a milestone for everyone. With proper planning, it can be an even more positive time of growth for the whole family.

REMEMBER WHEN *POT* WAS
something you cooked in and *bad* really meant bad, not good?

It's strange how some words pass in and out of common usage.
David Blankenhorn, the head of an organization that studies
cultural values, points out that the compliment "good family man"
is one of the phrases that has gone into obscurity.[13] It was once
widely used in our culture to designate a true badge of honor. The
rough translation would be: someone who puts his family first.

Look at the three words that make up that phrase. *Good:*
refers to widely accepted moral values. *Family:* points to purposes
larger than the self. And *man:* says there's a norm of masculinity.
It seems that contemporary culture no longer celebrates a widely
shared ideal of such a man who puts his family first.

Where do we see responsible masculinity represented on
television? Bill Cosby modeled it for a few years, but who else
has been portrayed in the media as a good family man? There just

aren't many. No, we're more likely to hear about superstar athletes or the ladies' man or the entrepreneur who's sacrificed all, including his wife and children, to make his start-up company a success.

Fortunately, it's not too late to bring this simple phrase back into vogue. "A good family man." It is indeed one of the highest callings to which a man can aspire.

IF MOTHERS WERE ASKED TO indicate the most irritating feature of child rearing, I'm convinced that sibling rivalry would get their overwhelming vote. Little children, and older ones, too, are not content just to hate each other in private. They attack one another like miniature warriors, arguing, fighting, hitting, screaming, and probing for weaknesses in the defensive line. It's enough to drive Mom and Dad up the wall.

But it doesn't have to be that way. It is neither necessary nor healthy to allow children to attack each other and make life miserable for the adults around them. You may not harmonize the kids' relationship entirely, but at least you can avoid making it worse. I recommend that parents be careful not to inflame the natural jealousies between children. Ever since time began, brothers and sisters have resented each other's successes and competed for parental attention. That's why mothers and fathers should be very careful to avoid casual comments that favor one of their kids over the others, especially in the areas of physical attractiveness, intelligence, and athletic ability.

Those are the three raw nerves on which self-esteem hangs in Western societies. To refer to a child as "my pretty daughter" or to a son as "the smart one" is to set off raging emotions in those who perceive themselves to be ugly or dumb. Sensitivity in those areas will reduce the antagonism between siblings and create a more harmonious tone for every member of the family.

You Always Bite the One You Love

ISN'T IT CURIOUS HOW IN THE midst of a nasty family argument we can shake out of the bad mood the instant the telephone rings or a neighbor knocks on the door?

Sometimes those we love are treated the worst, and kids are quick to notice this hypocrisy. Have you ever been brought up short by a small voice questioning this sudden turn to peaches and cream after twenty minutes of fire and brimstone?

Mark Hatfield, a longtime senator from Oregon and the father of four kids, said his wife stung him once by saying, "I just wish you were as patient with your children as you are with your constituents."

He isn't alone. We're all guilty at times of what I call "split vision," treating certain people with forbearance while heaping contempt on others under our own roof. We assume the worst; we pounce on every shortcoming. We never miss an opportunity to deliver a corrective harangue. And in the process, we wound the people we care about the most.

Isn't it time to cut one another a little slack at home? If, in fact, we love our spouses and our children and our parents as much as we say we do, one way to show it is to give them the kind words we bestow on our casual acquaintances.

Teens before Their Time

IS YOUR MAILBOX STUFFED WITH catalogs full of trendy designer clothes for every member of the family? Ours is. The other day I saw a pair of high-tech padded running shoes that cost nearly fifty dollars, and they were designed for toddlers who are barely able to walk.

More and more, we see adolescent clothes, attitudes, and values being marketed to younger and younger children. Those perfectly beautiful fashion dolls and the dating culture they inspire are aimed primarily at the elementary school-age market. Teenage stars, too, are promoted to the preteen set, which responds with appropriate crushes and fan mail. And rock and rap music, with adolescent and adult themes, is finding eager listeners among the very young.

This adolescent obsession can place our children on a very unnatural timetable, likely to reach the peak of sexual interest several years before it's due. That has obvious implications for their social and emotional health. I believe it is desirable to postpone the adolescent experience until it is summoned by the happy hormones. Therefore, I strongly recommend that parents screen the influences to which their children are exposed, keeping activities appropriate for each age.

While we can't isolate our kids from the world as it is, we don't have to turn our babies into teenyboppers.

The Toughest Hour of the Day

WHY IS THE EVENING DRIVE TIME in a big city called "the rush hour" when nothing moves? The real rush hour occurs when people arrive at home.

Early evening is a time when everyone is hungry and tempers are short. Two-career parents usually come home irritable and tired. But their children are unsympathetic and need immediate attention. It is a setup for conflict.

There are some things you can do to help defuse this rush-hour time bomb. First, you might want to telephone your children before you leave work in the afternoon. This can give you a head start in dealing with any troubles that might be brewing at home. Second, make a conscious effort during the commute to disengage from the responsibilities of the job. Listen to some "elevator music," and unwind from the cares of the day.

Concerning the dinner meal, it is wise to do as much as possible in the morning or the night before. Crock-Pot-type dinners that have cooked all day or those that can go straight from the refrigerator to the oven will relieve pressure at a time when stress is the greatest. The quicker everyone can eat and raise their blood sugar, the better. Then spend some time with the kids before homework and baths begin. You might take the dog on a neighborhood walk or play catch in the backyard. Finally, get the kids in bed and reserve a few moments of tranquillity for yourselves.

OK, let's admit it. There's no easy way to get through "rush hour" five nights a week, but with a little forethought, it can be less stressful.

MILLIONS OF ADULTS TODAY SUFFER from low self-esteem. Most of them learned to hate their bodies or their circumstances when they were in adolescence and continued at war with themselves into the adult years. It is self-imposed ridicule, and there are few experiences in life that are more destructive.

If you're among the vast number of people who have never come to terms with their own identity, let me offer a word of advice that may be helpful. The standards by which you have assessed yourself are themselves changing and fickle.

Dr. Maxwell Maltz, the plastic surgeon who authored *Psycho-Cybernetics,* said women came to him in the 1920s requesting that their breasts be reduced in size. More recently women wanted them augmented with silicone (until the health risks became understood).

False values!

In King Solomon's biblical love song, the bride asked her

groom to overlook her dark skin, which occurred from exposure to the sun. But today she'd be the pride of the beach.

False values!

Modern women are ashamed to admit that they carry an extra ten pounds of weight, yet Rembrandt would have loved to paint their plump bodies.

False values!

The standards by which we measure ourselves are arbitrary, temporary, and unfair. It's a system designed to undermine confidence. Your personal worth is not really dependent on the opinions of others or the fluctuating values that they represent. Every person alive is entitled to dignity, self-respect, and confidence.

The sooner you can accept the transcending worth of your humanness as a gift from God, the sooner you can rid yourself of the burden of low self-esteem.

Peace in the Neighborhood

IS THERE ANYTHING PARENTS CAN do about the misbehavior of other parents' children in a neighborhood? As a matter of fact, there is.

They can bring about a more peaceful atmosphere on their street if they will simply talk to each other—but that can take some doing. There is no quicker way to anger a mama bear than for someone to criticize her precious cub. That's a delicate subject indeed. And that's why the typical neighborhood provides very little feedback to parents in regard to the behavior of their children. The kids know there are no lines of communication between adults, and they take advantage of the barrier.

What each block needs is a mother or father who has the courage to say, "I want to be told what my child does when he's beyond his own yard. If he's a brat with other children, I would like to know it. If he's disrespectful with adults, please mention it to me. I won't consider it tattling. I won't resent your coming to me. I hope I can share my insights regarding your children, too."

As tough as it is to hear that our kids have misbehaved, because it makes us feel like bad parents, we should open ourselves to that information if it's valid. None of our kids is perfect. We'll know better how to teach and discipline them if we talk openly and honestly to each of our neighbors as adults and friends.

LET'S TALK ABOUT MONEY, WHICH is the most common source of conflict in marriage. Money is divisive because men and women typically have very different ideas about how it ought to be used. My father, for example, was an avid hunter, and he thought nothing of buying three boxes of shotgun shells to use in an afternoon of recreational shooting. Yet if my mother, who loved to shop, spent an equal amount of money on an extra potato peeler, he considered it wasteful. Never mind that she enjoyed browsing in stores as much as he enjoyed traipsing through the fields. His values were simply different from hers.

Another disagreement about money involves the decision about when and for what credit should be obtained. This is dangerous territory for husbands and wives. Nothing irritates a disciplined, frugal person more than having a spouse who squanders their resources, and their future earnings, for things that aren't needed.

These differences in perspective often surface during the honeymoon and become battlegrounds a few weeks later.

Accordingly, I'm convinced that the first principle of a healthy marriage is to stay out of debt and to be extremely careful with credit cards. Their misuse can undermine a family's financial stability, and they should be labeled "Danger! Handle with care!"

If money is a source of trouble in your family, sit down long enough to develop a plan on which you both agree, perhaps with the help of a financial counselor. It's the least you can do for one another.

ERMA BOMBECK ONCE WROTE, "The family that plays together, fights together," [14] and I'm afraid she was right.

Why is it that children are often the most obnoxious and irritating on vacations and at other times when parents specifically try to please them? On those special days, you'd think the kids would say to themselves, "Wow! Mom and Dad are doing something really nice for us, taking us on this great vacation. We're going to give them a break and be really good kids today."

Unfortunately, children just don't think that way. Why is this? One reason, I think, is because children often feel compelled to reexamine the boundaries whenever they think they may have moved. In other words, whenever the normal routine changes, kids often push the limits to see just what they can get away with.

So how can parents preserve their own peace of mind and

maintain harmony during car trips and family holidays? Well, sometimes it helps to redefine the boundaries at the beginning of your time together. Let the kids know exactly what you're doing and what's expected of them. If they still misbehave, respond with good, loving discipline right from the start.

No parent wants to be an ogre on vacation, but it helps to show a little firmness at the outset that can make the rest of the time together fun for the entire family.

IN THE 1960S, THE SURGEON general declared cigarettes harmful to the smoker's health. More recently, researchers have warned us about the dangers of foods high in fat and cholesterol. But something we hear less about are the health hazards of divorce.

Many studies have revealed the emotional and financial impact of divorce on couples and their children. But less well known is the research showing that divorce puts people at a high risk for psychiatric problems and physical disease.

Dr. David Larson, psychiatrist and researcher in Washington, D.C., reviewed medical studies on this subject and made some startling discoveries. For instance, being divorced and a nonsmoker is only slightly less dangerous than smoking a pack or more a day and staying married. Also, every type of terminal cancer strikes divorced individuals of both sexes more frequently than it does married people. What's more, premature death rates are significantly higher among divorced men and women. Physicians believe this is because the emotional trauma of divorce stresses the body and lowers the immune system's defense against disease.

In the light of this evidence, perhaps the surgeon general should consider warning married couples about the potential health risks of divorce. Certainly, healthy families are more beneficial to the well-being of children.

Beating the Doldrums

MANY MARRIAGES SEEM TO LOSE the wind in their romantic sails and drift aimlessly through the sea of matrimony.

Their plight reminds me of seamen back in the days of wooden vessels. Sailors in that era had much to fear, including pirates, storms, and diseases. But their greatest fear was that the ship might encounter the doldrums. The doldrums was an area of the ocean near the equator characterized by calm and very light shifting winds. It could mean death for the entire crew. The ship's food and water supply would be exhausted as they drifted for days, or even weeks, waiting for a breeze to put them back on course.

Well, marriages that were once exciting and loving can also get caught in the romantic doldrums, causing the relationship to die a slow and painful death. Author Doug Fields, in his book *Creative Romance,* writes, "Dating and romancing your spouse can change those patterns, and it can be a lot of fun. There's no quick fix to a stagnant marriage, of course, but you can lay aside the excuses and begin to date your sweetheart again."

It'll take a conscious effort to fill your sails again, but some creative ideas will help. How about breakfast in bed? a kiss in the rain? or rereading those old love letters?

The honeymoon need not be a forgotten experience.

Stress and the Human Body

I WONDER IF YOU'VE EVER HAD AN experience like the one I went through a few years ago. I had gone to bed early one night and was lying there waiting for my wife to finish some work in the kitchen. As she had loaded the dishwasher, I could hear its gentle *swoosh-swoosh*ing from the other end of the house. Then, suddenly, I realized that it wasn't the machine I was hearing at all. It was the squishy, rhythmic sound of my own heart—beating in my ear instead of in my chest where it belonged. This pounding went on for a week and began to drive me crazy.

I finally made an appointment with a specialist who told me that the muscles in my face were squeezing the vessels near my ear. I was actually hearing the blood trying to get past those constricted channels.

"It's not dangerous," I was told by the doctor.

"What would cause it?" I asked.

"It's stress," he told me. "You're running too fast."

I said, "I suppose you're going to tell me to slow down."

"Nope," he replied with a smile. "I can't control my own life. Why would I try to tell you how to manage yours?"

The doctor had it right. Stress is a fact of life in this high-speed culture. It can make your head hurt, your intestines retch, and your blood-pressure soar. It can even make your ears pound and squish in the night. Stress is the price we pay for being racehorses instead of cows.

But why do we live such hectic lives? What could possibly motivate us to run the human engine at full throttle until it threatens to blow up or melt down? I don't know, but I'm convinced that this kind of breathless living is an assault on common sense and good judgment. It not only threatens our physical bodies but is also the ultimate destroyer of meaningful family life.

Freedom and Independence

HOW DOES A CHILD LEARN TO handle freedom and independence? It ought to occur little by little as the years unfold. The goal is to prepare a child carefully for that moment of release when he or she is beyond the reach of the parent.

I learned this principle from my own mother, who made a calculated effort to teach independence and responsibility. After laying a foundation during the younger years, she gave me a "final examination" when I was seventeen years old. Mom and Dad went on a two-week trip and left me at home with the family car and permission to have my buddies stay at the house. Wow! Fourteen slumber parties in a row! I couldn't believe it. We could have gone crazy and torn the place apart, but we didn't. We behaved rather responsibly.

I always wondered why my mother took such a risk, and after I was grown, I asked her about it. She just smiled and said, "I knew in one year you would be leaving for college, where you would have complete freedom with no one watching over you. I wanted to expose you to that independence while you were still under my influence."

You see, my mother employed an important child-rearing principle in that instance. For years she had been consciously preparing me for the coming independence.

If you have children, let them test the waters of freedom as they're growing up, rather than thrusting them into the big wide ocean all at once. Then when they're on their own and completely emancipated, they'll know how to handle the experience responsibly and wisely.

Ordinary Kids

WHEN THE BIRTH OF A FIRSTBORN child is imminent, his parents pray that he will be normal; that is average. But from that moment on, average will not be good enough.

Their child must excel. He must succeed. He must triumph. He must be the first of his age to walk or talk or ride a tricycle. He must earn a stunning report card and amaze his teachers with his wit and wisdom. He must star in Little League, and later he must be quarterback or senior class president or valedictorian. His sister must be the cheerleader or the soloist or the homecoming queen. Throughout the formative years of childhood, his parents give him the same message day after day: "We're counting on you to do something fantastic, Son. Now don't disappoint us."

Unfortunately, exceptional children are just that . . . exceptions. Seldom does a five-year-old memorize the King James Version of the Bible, or play chess blindfolded, or compose symphonies in the Mozart manner. To the contrary, the vast majority of our children are not dazzlingly brilliant, extremely witty, highly coordinated, tremendously talented, or universally popular. They are just plain kids with oversized needs to be loved and accepted as they are.

Most parents have average kids, and to expect more sets the stage for considerable disappointment for parents and puts unrealistic pressure on the younger generation.

A Word about Parental Guilt

IN CASE YOU HAVEN'T NOTICED, parenthood is a very guilt-producing endeavor, even for the dedicated professional.

Since there's no such creature as a perfect parent, we subject ourselves to a constant cross-examination in the courtroom of parental acceptability. Was my discipline fair? Did I overreact out of frustration and anger? Have I been partial to the child who's my secret favorite? Have I made the same mistakes for which I resented my own parents? Round and round go the self-doubts and recriminations, and guilt becomes a constant companion, especially for those whose kids are grown and whose record is already in the books.

The best way to handle parental guilt is to face it squarely, using it as a source of motivation for change where it's warranted. I would suggest that mothers and fathers sit down together and discuss their feelings. Write down the most troubling shortcomings. Then ask, "Is our guilt valid? Can we do anything about it? If so, what? If not, isn't it appropriate that we lay the matter to rest?"

Remember that we can no more be perfect parents than we can be perfect human beings. We get tired, frustrated, disappointed, and irritable, which necessarily affects the way we approach those little ones around our feet. Fortunately, we are permitted to make many mistakes through the years, provided the overall tone is somewhere near the right note.

A PARENT WHO SEES THE UNMIS-
takable signs of adolescence beginning to arrive in a son or daughter
needs to set aside some time for a final all-important conversation.

In many ways, the parent of a preteen has a task similar to
a football coach who has trained his squad all through the late
summer and early fall. Finally the first game is about to occur,
when direct coaching is not going to be possible. He gathers the
kids in the locker room and makes one last speech before they
take the field. He reminds them of the fundamentals and gives
them the old pep talk about winning.

In a similar way, parents of preteens have been teaching
their youngsters all through preschool and the elementary years.
They've been teaching about right and wrong, what they believe,
and how to behave. There's so much that they need to summarize
in this pep talk. Soon the big contest called adolescence will begin

and the teen will take the field. From that point forward, very little parental advice can be given.

That's why I recommend that parents take an eleven- or twelve-year-old child on a "preparing for adolescence" trip, during which moral values and the family's principles are repeated and emphasized. Sex education and the physical changes of adolescence, the approaching social pressures, and other fundamentals should be discussed.

That conversation should end with a Knute Rockne inspirational message—giving them a loving hug and sending the "team" onto the field. Then hold your breath and pray like crazy.

Love Is Having to Say "I'm Sorry"

MANY PEOPLE HAVE A HARD
time saying that they're sorry to anyone, let alone to their children, but there are times when it's the only thing to do. Apologizing when we're wrong provides opportunities to teach valuable lessons to our sons and daughters.

I remember one evening after a very hard day of work when I was especially grouchy with my ten-year-old daughter. After going to bed that night, I just felt like I hadn't treated her right and that I needed to ask her for forgiveness. So before she left for school the next morning, I said, "Honey, I know that you know that daddies aren't perfect, and I have to admit that I wasn't fair with you last night. I want you to forgive me." She put her arms around my neck, and she shocked me down to my toes. She said, "I knew you were gonna have to say that, Daddy, and it's OK. I forgive you."

Like my daughter, most children are very resilient, and

they're eager to reconcile. Although you may have to sputter out the words, asking a child for forgiveness when you're wrong shows that you have flaws and imperfections like everyone else. And it models apologetic behavior for them.

In the family where no apologies are offered, problems are often swept under the rug. But by saying "I'm sorry" you can bring a world of healing and calm to an irritable and stressed-out household. It's a humbling experience, to be sure, but we can all stand a little unscheduled humility.

Learning to Write Right

VERY FEW CHILDREN LEARN TO write adequately today, but it's a skill worth emphasizing at home.

The early development of my own writing career, which now includes more than twenty books, began when I was in elementary school. My parents encouraged me and helped me grow in this area. I remember writing a letter to a friend when I was nine years old. My mother then sat down with me and suggested that we read it together. I started the letter, "Dear Tom, how are you? I am just fine." My mom asked me if I thought that sounded a little boring. She said, "You haven't said anything. You used a few words, but they have no meaning." I never wrote that phrase again, although that is the typical way a child begins a letter.

Looking back, I can see how, even at an early age, my mother was teaching me to write. It's not terribly difficult or time-consuming to encourage and teach kids some of the fundamentals. One approach is to ask a family member to correspond with your child and encourage him to write back. Then when your child shows you his reply, sprinkle a few corrections, like my mother offered, with a generous portion of praise. And then entice him to do a little creative expression.

It's also helpful to have a few English teachers who will invest themselves in a budding young writer. I had one in high school and another in college who were determined to teach me grammar and composition. They nearly beat me to death, but I earn a living today with the skills they gave me. Especially, I would like to say thanks to Dr. Ed Harwood. His classes were like marine boot camp, but what I learned there was priceless.

The ability to write has gone out of style—much like the old "homemaking" classes for girls. But it is an incredibly valuable craft that your child can use in a wide variety of settings. Don't let him grow up without developing it.

TEACHING CHILDREN TO APPRECIATE nature is one of the most enjoyable tasks of parenting. It's also one of the simplest, since children are naturally curious about the world around them.

When I was very young, I had a fascination with red ants. We had a big two-gallon fruit jar that I used for an ant farm. I'd fill it with dirt, then collect thousands of red ants and put them inside. I'd keep them for months at a time, watching them dig chambers and compartments and trails. Apart from being stung a few hundred times, it was a successful project. And it helped instill in me a sense of wonder at nature and creation that has continued to this day.

When you start teaching your own child about nature, I suggest you capitalize on her own curiosity. If she walks into the house with an earthworm or a frog in her hand, see it as an opportunity. Our own two-year-old once asked his mother if worms could yawn. She was unprepared for the inquiry.

If you have a backyard, walk around with your child and look under the leaves and rocks just to see what you can find. Even in a small window box, you can grow a garden and teach the miracle of plant life from seed to harvest. It only takes a little effort to kindle in your child a lasting fascination with the beauty of the natural world.

The Battle for Control

EVERYBODY UNDERSTANDS THAT
teenagers are itching to get out on their own—to run their own lives
and not have parents telling them what to do anymore. But this
yearning for control actually starts much earlier. It's a fundamental
dimension of the human personality.

I remember one mother of a tough little four-year-old girl who
was demanding her own way. The mother said, "Now, Jenny,
you're just going to have to obey me. I'm your boss, and I have
the responsibility to lead you, and that's what I intend to do!"

Little Jenny thought over her mother's words for a minute,
and then she said, "How long does it have to be that way?"

Already at four years of age, this child was yearning for a day
of freedom when nobody could tell her what to do. Something
deep within her spirit was reaching out for control. She shares that
yearning with millions of her age-mates—some more than others.
The task for us as parents is to hang on to the reins of authority in

the early days, even though little hands are trying to pry our fingers loose, and then gradually grant independence as maturity arrives. But this is the most delicate responsibility in parenting. Power granted too early produces folly, but power granted too late brings rebellion.

It is a wise mother or father who can let go little by little as the growing child is able to stand on his or her own. If you watch and listen carefully, the critical milestones will be obvious.

A No-Knock Policy

ONE OF THE MOST COMMON characteristics of a person who feels inadequate and inferior is that he talks about his deficiencies to anyone who will listen.

For example, an overweight person feels compelled to apologize to his companions for ordering a hot-fudge sundae. He echoes what he imagines they're already thinking. "I'm fat enough without eating this," he says, scooping up the cherry and the syrup with his spoon. Likewise, a woman who thinks she's unintelligent will admit freely, "I'm really bad at math. I can hardly add two plus two."

This kind of self-denigration is not as uncommon as one might think. Listen to yourself in the weeks to come. You might be surprised by how often you emphasize your faults to your friends. While you're babbling about all of your inadequacies, the listener is formulating his impressions of you. He will later see you and treat you according to the evidence that you've provided. After all, you're the expert on that subject.

This understanding is particularly important for children, who should be taught what I call a "no-knock policy" by their parents. Kids should learn that constant self-ridicule can simply become a bad habit.

There's a big difference between accepting blame when it's valid and simply chattering about one's inferiority. It really boils down to this—self-respect breeds respect among others. Children are fully capable of understanding that fact.

The Security of Boundaries

CHILDREN FEEL MORE SECURE,
and therefore tend to flourish, when they know where the boundaries
are. Let me illustrate that principle.

Imagine you're driving a car over the Royal Gorge Bridge in
Colorado, which is suspended hundreds of feet above the canyon
floor. As a first-time traveler, you're pretty tense as you drive
across. It is a scary experience. I knew one little fellow who
was so awed by the view over the side of the bridge that he said,
"Wow, Daddy! If you fell off of here, it'd kill you constantly!"

Now suppose there were no guardrails on the side of the
bridge. Where would you steer the car? Right down the middle
of the road. Even though you don't plan to hit those protective
railings along the side, you just feel more secure knowing that
they're there.

It's the same way with children. There is security in defined
limits. They need to know precisely what the rules are and who's

available to enforce them. When these clear boundaries exist at home, the child lives in utter safety. He never gets in trouble unless he deliberately asks for it. And as long as he stays within those reasonable, well-marked guardrails, there's mirth and freedom and acceptance.

Your children need the security of defined limits, too. They may not admit that they want you to be the boss, but they breathe easier when you are.

IF YOU WANT TO PUT SOME NEW
life in your marriage, try thinking like a teenager again.

We all remember, fondly or otherwise, the craziness of our
dating days. The coy attitudes, the flirting, the fantasies, the
chasing after the prize. As we moved from courtship into marriage,
most of us felt we should grow up and leave the game playing
behind. But we may not have matured as much as we'd like to
think.

In truth, our romantic relationships will always bear some
characteristics of adolescent sexuality. Adults still love the thrill
of the chase, the lure of the unattainable, the excitement of the
new and boredom with the old. Immature impulses are controlled
and minimized in a committed relationship, of course, but they
never fully disappear.

This might be a key to keeping vitality in your marriage. If
things seem stale between you and your spouse, maybe you should

remember some old tricks. Maybe it's time for a little mystery, a little flirtatiousness, a date where you revisit the places you enjoyed when your love was new and relive some of the happy moments that brought you together.

If it sounds a little immature to act like a teenager again, just keep this in mind: In the best marriages, the chase is never really over.

My Kid's a Superstar

HOW DO YOU FEEL ABOUT THOSE bumper stickers that say, "My Child Is an Honor Student at Washington Junior High School"? I imagine they are irritating to parents whose kids are less gifted. One such mother put this sticker on her car: "My Kid Can Beat Up Your Honor Student."

We all feel good about the successes of our children, and well we should. Problems arise, however, when the pride of the family is riding on the shoulders of an immature child. Boys and girls should know that they're accepted simply because of their own unique worth.

I'm reminded of John McKay, the former great football coach at the University of Southern California. I saw him interviewed on television some years ago when his son John Jr. was a successful football player on the USC team. The interviewer asked Coach McKay to comment on the pride he must have felt over his son's accomplishments. His answer was most impressive.

"Yes," he said, "I'm pleased that John has had a good season this year. He does a fine job, and I'm proud of him. But I would be just as proud if he had never played the game at all."

Coach McKay was saying, in effect, that John's football talent is recognized and appreciated, but his human worth does not depend on his ability to play football. Thus, his son would not lose his respect if the next season brought failure and disappointment. John's place in his dad's heart was secure, independent of his performance.

I wish every child could say the same.

How Tough Is Parenting?

A FEW YEARS AGO I ASKED ONE thousand mothers and fathers to describe their greatest frustrations in raising kids. I heard many humorous stories in response about sticky telephones and wet toilet seats and knotted shoestrings. One mother actually wanted to know why toddlers never throw up in the bathroom. To do so would violate an unwritten law of the universe, to be sure.

But in our poll, parents didn't merely laugh about their frustrations—they tended to blame themselves. They said they were overwhelmed and were losing confidence in their ability to do the job. Many were having trouble just coping from day to day. How sad it is that this ancient responsibility of raising children has become so burdensome and laden with guilt.

Actually, the facts won't support that self-condemnation in the majority of cases. Most moms and dads are doing a credible job at home. And it's time that someone patted them on the back for their commitment and their sacrifice. And someday, when the frustrations of toddlerhood and the turmoil of adolescence have passed, they'll enjoy the sweet benefits of being very good and loving parents.

Hang in there, moms and dads. You're more skilled than you think you are.

Flattery versus Praise

IT IS GOOD TO PRAISE CHILDREN FOR the responsible things they do, but should there be a limit to the compliments we offer them?

Affirmation is essential to children's self-esteem, and they develop best when they get plenty of it. But too many good words heaped on kids for the wrong reasons can be inflationary and unhealthy for them. This empty rhetoric is called flattery, which differs from praise in that it is unearned. Flattery is what Grandma offers when she comes for a visit and says, "Oh, what a beautiful little girl you are! You're getting prettier every day," or, "My, what a smart boy you are. Aren't you big?"

Let me say it again. Flattery occurs when compliments are showered on a child for something that is unrelated to effort, achievement, or maturity. Praise, on the other hand, is a genuine reaction to the good things that a child has done.

To be effective, praise should be very specific. "You've been a good boy" is too general. Much better is "I like the way you cleaned your room today" or "I'm proud of the way you studied for that math assignment last night." You see, praise reinforces the child's constructive behavior. It rewards him or her for doing something positive and valuable, and increases the chances that it will recur.

As parents, we should be on the lookout for opportunities to offer genuine, well-deserved praise to our children while avoiding the emptiness of flattery.

The Wrenching Task of Letting Go

ONE OF THE MOST DIFFICULT responsibilities parents face is the task of letting go.

When children are young, Mom and Dad are busy providing love, protection, and authority for them. It seems as though those responsibilities will go on forever. But very quickly, their sons and daughters reach the late teens and early twenties when the door must be fully opened to the world outside. It's the most frightening time of parenthood.

The tendency is to retain control in order to prevent the budding young adults from making mistakes. However, our grown kids are more likely to make the proper choices if they aren't forced to rebel in order to gain their freedom. The simple truth is that responsibility and maturity thrive best in an atmosphere of freedom.

One further word of advice should be offered. A sudden release from all parental guidance and direction at the end of childhood carries dangerous implications. We've all seen individuals who went a little crazy when they were put on their own for the first time. It's much better to grant independence little by little, through the years, as our kids are able to handle a new responsibility. The final release, then, should represent a small step toward freedom rather than a tumble off the cliff into anarchy.

The goal is simple. We need to cut loose the strings of authority little by little so that when our children are beyond the reach of our authority, they no longer need it.

A Better Way of Moving On

MOVING TO A NEW SCHOOL OR A
new city can be a threatening experience for children, but there
are some ways to make the transfer easier.

Preparation and forethought are the keys. Educator Cheri
Fuller recommends that those who are about to relocate call a
family meeting to talk about what's about to happen. Begin to
lay plans together. It's sad to say good-bye to good friends, and
it's hard to make new ones. Try establishing pen pals for your
children in the new school long before the move is to occur.
Relationships can blossom through the mail so that the kids are
not entirely unknown in the new location.

It's also good to create curiosity about the new city or neighborhood you're moving to. Write to the state tourist bureau or to the
chamber of commerce and ask for brochures and maps. When your
children begin to see some of the adventure of moving, they may
develop a more positive attitude toward leaving.

A bit of preparation and a healthy dose of communication can help clear the way for a smoother journey to a new home.

A Word for Alcoholics

A COMPANY PRESIDENT WAS ASKED to fill out a government form that asked, "How many employees do you have—broken down by sex?" He replied, "None that I know of. Our big problem here is alcohol."

Actually, the problem of alcoholism in our society is no laughing matter, especially when you consider the havoc that's wreaked by this addiction. But how does one know when he or she has crossed the line from being a social drinker to being a full-blown alcoholic?

The first red flag is a tolerance for alcohol. The person finds that he has to drink more to achieve the same result. He brags about being able to "hold" his liquor—as though that were something to be proud of. In reality, showing a tolerance for booze is a dangerous indicator that a chemical adjustment has been made.

Secondly, the alcoholic doesn't want to talk about his drinking. This is the beginning of denial that may be with him for years to come. Next, he begins to experience blackouts. And finally, he is helpless to control how much he drinks once he gets started.

If that profile describes you or a loved one, don't waste another day. Call Alcoholics Anonymous or a center that specializes in treating this disease. You and your family will never regret taking that first step toward recovery.

EVERY YEAR AN ASTOUNDING NUMBER of marriages disintegrate and leave deeply wounded people in their wake. But why is the casualty rate so high? One reason is the tendency for young men and women to marry virtual strangers. It's true that a typical couple talks for countless hours during the courtship period, and they believe they know each other intimately. But a dating relationship is designed to conceal information, not reveal it. Consequently, the bride and groom often enter into marriage with an array of private and conflicting opinions about how life's going to be lived after the wedding, and the stage is set for serious confrontations.

For this reason I strongly believe that each engaged couple should participate in at least six to eight sessions with a competent marriage counselor in order to identify the assumptions that each partner holds and to work through areas of potential conflict. When this occurs, some couples discover that they have unresolvable differences, and they agree to either postpone or call off the wedding. Others work through their conflicts and proceed toward marriage with increased confidence.

Either way, getting better acquainted before marriage is strategic. If by doing so we can reduce the tragedy of divorce by even 5 percent, it would certainly be worth the effort.

Green Runway Lights

WHEN I'M FLYING INTO LOS Angeles International Airport at night, I sometimes look ahead to see the green runway lights that tell the captain where to land the plane. Captains know that if they bring their craft down between those boundaries, all should be well. In a similar way, parents need some runway lights—some guiding principles—that will help them raise their children. Without a beacon or two to direct their flight, they're blindly approaching a very complex and important task.

There are two fundamental principles that might be thought of as beacons to guide the parenting assignment. The first is to assure our kids that they are loved unconditionally. Without that awareness, little people wither like plants without water. The second is less understood but equally important. It requires us to teach our kids to respect parental authority. The child's acceptance of benevolent leadership, beginning at home, sets the stage for his attitude toward other forms of authority later in life. These two components, love and authority, are basic to the developmental needs of children.

By heeding these guiding lights on the runway, your child has a good chance of making a successful flight and a safe landing beyond the turbulence of adolescence.

I SPOKE AT A WHITE HOUSE conference a few years ago during which the other speaker was Dr. Armand Nicholi, a psychiatrist from Harvard University. His topic, like mine, was the status of the American family.

Dr. Nicholi explained how an overcommitted lifestyle that makes parents inaccessible to their children produces much the same effect as divorce itself, and herein lies our most serious failing as mothers and fathers. Cross-cultural studies make it clear that parents in the United States spend less time with their children than parents in almost any other nation in the world. For decades, fathers have devoted themselves exclusively to their occupations and activities away from home. More recently, mothers have joined the workforce in huge numbers, rendering themselves exhausted at night and burdened with domestic duties on weekends. The result: No one is at home to meet the needs of lonely preschoolers and latchkey children. Dr. Nicholi expressed regret that his comments would make many parents feel uncomfortable and guilty. However, he felt obligated to report the facts as he saw them.

Most important, Dr. Nicholi stressed as the point of his address the undeniable link between the interruption of parent-child relationships and the escalation of psychiatric problems that we were then seeing. If the trend continued, he said, serious national health problems were inevitable. One-half of all hospital beds in the United States at that time were taken up by psychiatric patients. That figure could hit 95 percent if the incidence of divorce, child abuse, child molestation, and child neglect continues to soar. In that event, we'll also see vast increases in teen suicide, already up more than 300 percent in twenty-five years, and drug abuse, crimes of violence, and problems related to sexual disorientation.

WE'VE WRITTEN ABOUT DIVORCE'S lifelong consequences for children. But what about parent-child separation that occurs for reasons other than divorce? Is the pain any less intense for kids when the disruptive factors are unrelated to family disintegration?

Research confirms that the consequences of *any* parent-child separation are severe. In one study of fathers whose jobs required them to be away from their families for long periods of time, the children tended to experience numerous negative reactions, including anger, rejection, depression, low self-esteem, and, commonly, a decline in school performance. Those findings have been confirmed in other contexts as well.

I have reason to understand the pain brought by family separation, because I experienced it when I was six years old. My mother and father left me with my aunt for six months while they traveled. I sat on my mother's lap while she told me how much she loved me and that she and my father would come back for me as soon as they could. Then they drove away as the sun dropped below the horizon. I sat on the floor in the dark for an unknown period of time, fighting back the tears that engulfed me. That sorrowful evening was so intense that its pain can be recalled instantly today, more than five decades later.

In short, even when parent-child separation occurs for valid reasons in a loving home, a boy or girl frequently interprets parental departure as evidence of rejection. Nothing short of necessity should cause us to put children through that experience.

The Great Safe-Sex Scam

FOR MORE THAN TWO DECADES, THE federal government has spent nearly three billion dollars to promote safe-sex ideology among American teenagers. It's time we asked what taxpayers have gotten for their money and what sex-education programs have achieved by such a massive effort.

In the 1970s, there were two sexually transmitted diseases (STDs) at epidemic proportions in this country, syphilis and gonorrhea. Both were entirely curable by brief antibiotic therapy. Today, more than twenty STDs infect large percentages of the population. Some of them, notably gonorrhea, are becoming resistant to most antibiotics and may soon be beyond the reach of medical science.

Of even greater concern are numerous sexually transmitted viruses, which now infect more than fifty million people. They include herpes, human papillomavirus (HVP), HIV, and AIDS-related illnesses. There is *no* cure for any of these diseases. Those who have them, which includes one in five Americans, will suffer for the rest of their lives! Many will ultimately succumb to their ravages.

There has been a conspiracy of silence about the dangers of these diseases. How many young women know, for example, that four thousand deaths per year are attributed to HPV?[15] Yet it is a known fact that condoms do not protect against this virus. It is transmitted from genital areas not protected by condoms. A year-long study of female students visiting the medical center at the University of California, Berkeley, showed that 47 percent of them were infected![16]

This is the legacy of an insane policy. Young people are suffering because the truth has been withheld from them. Those who depend on condoms to protect them during promiscuous sex usually wind up sick, pregnant, or both.

Without question, the safe-sex program is a disaster in the making!

Christmas Memories

WITHOUT A DOUBT, THE BEST TIME of the year for shared memories is Christmas. Some of my happiest memories, both as a child and as an adult, have been rooted in the Christmas season. I remember the year my father went to the bank and bought twenty new, crisp one-dollar bills back in the days when a dollar would buy a meal. He attached a Merry Christmas note to each dollar and handed them out; one apiece to the newsboy, the shoeshine man, the postman, and seventeen others. He was merely thanking them for being his friends.

Another memory occurred many years later. My wife, two children, and I had boarded a plane for Kansas City to spend the holidays with my parents. When I stepped off the plane and into the terminal, I instantly caught sight of my six-foot-four-inch father towering over the crowd. There was a twinkle in his eyes and a smile on his face, and Mom, of course, was aglow with excitement. Her family had come home for Christmas. That scene is videotaped in my mind today. Now those good people are gone, and only the memory lingers on.

During the Christmas season, I hope your own times of excitement and sharing and fellowship will leave you with a special gift . . . memories that will last a lifetime.

Of Balloons and Children

SEVERAL YEARS AGO I ATTENDED A wedding ceremony in a beautiful garden setting, and I came away with some thoughts on child rearing.

After the minister had instructed the groom to kiss the bride on that day, approximately one hundred and fifty colorful, helium-filled balloons were released into the blue California sky. Within a few seconds the balloons were scattered all across the heavens, some of them rising hundreds of feet overhead and others cruising toward the horizon. A few balloons struggled to clear the upper branches of the trees while the show-offs became mere pinpoints of color on their journey across the sky.

How interesting, I thought, and how symbolic of children. Let's face it—some boys and girls seem to be born with more helium than others. They catch all the right breezes, and they soar effortlessly to the heights, while others wobble dangerously close to the trees. Their frantic folks run along underneath, huffing and puffing to keep them airborne. It is an exhausting experience.

I want to offer a word of encouragement specifically to the parents of those low-flying kids. Sometimes the child who has the greatest trouble getting off the ground eventually soars to the highest heights. That's why I urge you as parents not to look too quickly for the person your child will become.

E N D N O T E S

1. Used by permission.
2. Tim Friend, "Heart Disease Awaits Today's Soft-Living Kids," *USA Today,* November 15, 1994, p.10.
3. Elise F. Jones and Jacqueline Darroch Forest, "Contraceptive Failure in the United States: Revised Estimates from the 1982 National Survey of Family Growth," *Family Planning Perspectives* (21), May/June 1989, p. 103.
4. *Ibid.,* 105.
5. Used by permission.
6. *Family Circle,* February 26, 1985.
7. J.S. Wallerstein and J. B. Kelley, "Effects of Divorce on the Visiting Father/Child Relationship," *American Journal of Psychiatry,* December 1980.
8. Dr. Archibald Hart, Fuller Theological Seminary, Pasadena, California.
9. *Focus on the Family,* December 20, 1982.
10. Sandra Boodman, "Researchers Study Obesity in Children," *Washington Post,* June 13, 1995, p. 210.
11. *Cradles of Eminence* is out of print; however, the information can be found in the following: Mildred G. Goertzel, *Three Hundred Eminent Personalities* (San Francisco: Jossey-Bass Publishers).

12. Harvard University Preschool Project, directed by Dr. Burton White, 1965-1975.

13. David Blankenhorn, "The Good Family Man: Fatherhood and the Pursuit of Happiness in America," An Institute for American Values Working Paper for the Symposium on Fatherhood in America, *Institutes for American Values*, November 1991.

14. Erma Bombeck, "The Family That Plays Together Gets on Each Other's Nerves," (New York: Warner Communications, 1978).

15. "Factors Associated with Human Papillomarvirus Infection in Women Encountered in Community-Based Offices," Barbara Reed, M.D., M.S.P.H., et al., *Archives of Family Medicine*, Vol.2., Dec. 1993, p. 1239.

16. "Genital HPV Infection in Female Universty Students as Determined by a PCR-Based Method," Heidi M. Bauer, *Journal of American Medical Association*, Vol. 265, No. 472, p. 1991.

INDEX